CREATING INDEPENDENT STUDENT LEARNERS

A PRACTICAL GUIDE TO ASSESSMENT FOR LEARNING

Pauline Clarke, Thompson Owens, Ruth Sutton

PORTAGE & MAIN PRESS

Portage and Main Press acknowledges the financial support of the Government of Canada through the Book Publishing Industry Development Program (BPIDP) for our publishing activities.

Cover and text design: Relish Design Studio LTD.
Cover photo: RubberBall Productions
Printed and bound in Canada by Friesens

Library and Archives Canada Cataloguing in Publication

Clarke, Pauline, 1947-
    Creating independent student learners, grade: N-3: a practical guide
to assessment for learning / Pauline Clarke, Thompson Owens, Ruth Sutton.

Includes bibliographical references.
ISBN 1-55379-086-3

    1. School children--Rating of. I. Owens, Thompson, 1947-
II. Sutton, Ruth, 1948- III. Title.

LB3060.22.C552 2006   372.126   C2006-904220-9

ISBN-10: 1-55379-086-3
ISBN-13: 978-1-55379-086-0

PORTAGE & MAIN PRESS

100 – 318 McDermot Ave.
Winnipeg, MB Canada R3A 0A2

Email: books@portageandmainpress.com
Tel: 204-987-3500
Toll-free: 1-800-667-9673
Toll-free fax: 1-866-734-8477

Mixed Sources

Cert no. SW-COC-001271
© 1996 FSC

FSC

To all the teachers of the

Winnipeg School Division

Inner City who are not

named in this book, but

who worked diligently as

we all tried to find the

best ways to help our

students succeed.

Acknowledgments

The authors wish to thank the Winnipeg School Division for permission to publish this material and, in particular, Mr. Jack Smyth, Chief Superintendent, Winnipeg School Division (1982–2002), who provided encouragement and support for the work described herein.

CONTENTS

INTRODUCTION

This book is about practical ways to help students become independent learners through *assessment for learning*. The ideas presented here come from an initiative to bring research on assessment into the classroom. During the years 2000 to 2003, 80 teachers from the Inner City District of Winnipeg School Division were given the opportunity to develop their skills in assessing their students. These teachers understood that assessment was an important part of their programs and were willing to explore their own practices and seek ways to improve. We named the project on assessment for learning *Feedback for Learning.*

This book is a showcase of the participating teachers who taught in grades N–3 classrooms, and of their experiences with reworking their assessment practices. Along with an abundance of information about how to create independent student learners, there are many comments and examples of their observations working with students. The eight steps in the scaffolding outlined in chapter 1 and expanded on in the remaining three chapters will give teachers a guide to how to rework their assessment practice and how to think about transforming their students into independent learners. Each chapter includes rubrics, working charts, and essays, themed according to our experiences with Feedback for Learning.

In addition to the practical information on creating independent learners, we believe it is important to share some of the thoughts and challenges we encountered, in part, to allow you to see that change in any teacher's practice is gradual; it takes more time than most of us would like, but it is worth the effort. We have included essays, our reflections, to help teachers feel more comfortable and confident as they embark on the process of change.

This book can be used independently by teachers, or as the basis of a study group with small groups of colleagues. Teachers may use the whole book as a program or they may read short sections to find effective ideas that will improve student performance. The book is organized around eight steps, structured into a scaffolding format. Each step is explained and there are examples of applications from participating teachers. We have also included ideas that helped teachers as they worked through the scaffolding to try to create independent student learners. We have divided the content into the steps in the scaffolding to help build the language, experiences, and thinking skills that students need in order to be reflective learners. The students become learners as they learn to identify their strengths, weaknesses, and strategies they can use to help themselves.

This is also a book about change. We believe that asking teachers to reflect on their practice and to implement new techniques in assessment are not trivial tasks. Classrooms are very complex places and teachers must be treated as adult learners. As you read through the book, you will see that teachers were encouraged to control the pace of their work, to discuss their ideas, to deepen their understanding, and to trust their intuitions.

The path for participating teachers was not always easy but their skill, perseverance, dedication, and good humour have resulted in a deeper understanding of how to help students become independent learners and of how to improve their students' performance.

1

KEY QUESTIONS

Assessment asks not only does the student self-assess but also does he/she self-adjust?

—Wiggins, 1998

Guiding Question

What impact does your present assessment program have on your students?

Key Ideas of Chapter One

- assessment for learning helps students use information about their own learning
- the goal of assessment for learning is to help students become independent learners
- the scaffolding is a frame of essential teacher behaviours for assessment for learning
- teachers must see themselves as learners in the change process

Introduction: Why Read This Book?

If you want to learn how to help students from nursery school to grade 3 become independent learners, the steps outlined in the following chapters will help. One of the charms of teaching students at these grade levels is that, by and large, they are completely open in their desire to learn from the teacher. It is also true that students at this age often seem to act in a random, self-centred manner. Teachers of students from nursery school to grade 3 know the absolute importance of routines for activities and the transitions between them.

While constant repetition and the establishment of order are essential, this book shows teachers how to go beyond classrooms that are just well-ordered to classrooms in which students are acquiring the self-knowledge that allows them to be powerful independent learners. In the following chapters, teachers will see how to set targets for their students' learning so that even the students who always seem to struggle, those who need the most help, will make substantial progress. Teachers work hard in the classroom to make sure all their students feel accepted. The tools and procedures outlined in the following pages will help students improve their performance and also help them recognize their success and talk about it. Students' awareness of their success means that their self-esteem rises as well.

This book will also help teachers who feel they are always being told, "If you would just do these 5, 10, 20 more things, your students will be successful." This is not a book about doing more to achieve success, but doing something different to create independent learners. When a teacher undertakes to re-examine their classroom practice, they should be aware that while the process is exciting and rewarding, change also takes time, patience, and support. Teachers must learn how to slow down. In this book, teachers will be introduced to a way of thinking about their work so they can become more efficient.

We do not promise miracles. But we can promise fewer days of being frazzled by the almost impossible task of reaching all the students all the time. We can also promise wonderful moments where you will be able to stand back and enjoy your students as learners.

What We Mean by *Assessment*

In the past few years, writers such as Black and Wiliam (1998), Stiggins (1997), and Davies (2000), have talked about feedback, assessment of learning, assessment for learning, and so on. Each writer places a slightly different emphasis on the meaning of the term *assessment*. In light of so many assessment ideas, it is particularly important to understand what we mean by assessment. We have broken the discussion of assessment into two basic areas:

- The first category of assessment is what we call *assessment of learning*. Most teachers understand assessment as the collection of data on students through tests, quizzes, and assignments. The teacher then uses the information as the basis for a term/semester evaluation, or grade. This information can also be used by teachers to decide what the students understand and what requires more attention. Teachers can then adjust their teaching program to help the students succeed. When the flow of the information about student performance is directed mostly towards the teacher, we distinguish this type of assessment as assessment of learning (see figure 1.1). This is an important aspect of a teacher's work, but assessment of learning is not the major concern of this book.

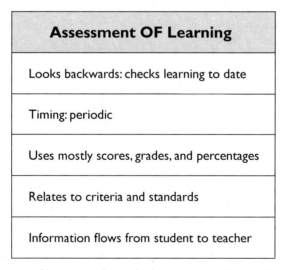

Assessment OF Learning

Looks backwards: checks learning to date

Timing: periodic

Uses mostly scores, grades, and percentages

Relates to criteria and standards

Information flows from student to teacher

Figure 1.1 Assessment of learning – flow of information to the teacher only.

- The second category of assessment, and the focus of this book, is *assessment for learning*. Students learn how to look carefully at their own work so they judge where they have been successful and where their work could improve. Students develop their own abilities to learn (see figure 1.2).

Assessment FOR Learning
Looks forwards: used to decide next steps in learning and teaching
Timing: continual
Uses specific words to provide feedback
Relates to student's progress
Information flows between student and teacher

Figure 1.2 Assessment for learning – information about performance to the student and teacher.

We want to expand teachers' thinking from *assessment of learning*, where the data about progress are used primarily by themselves, to *assessment for learning*, with procedures that help students learn how to use information about their own learning. Using assessment for learning can create classrooms where both the teacher and students are able to use feedback to adjust their performance. The teacher uses feedback to adjust the teaching and the students use feedback to adjust their learning.

In our approach to assessment, teachers acquire a process that can be incorporated into all their daily routines. The activities and suggestions are presented as part of a whole, and the emphasis is on teacher observation and the daily conversations between teacher and students that build the students' knowledge about how they learn and how they can improve. We also stress the need for students to develop a language of learning so that their understanding of themselves as learners, and their ability to talk about themselves as learners, develop in a complementary way.

For young students at the beginning of their school years and their teachers, assessment for learning may seem daunting. Students in the primary grades do not arrive in class with the ability to assess themselves. Teachers we worked with have, however, found that even at this early stage, students can be guided to see themselves as learners and become more successful. The ability to reflect on personal performance is a thinking skill all students can acquire. Starting early gives students the best opportunity to develop and refine this essential aspect of being a successful learner.

In this book, when we use the term *assessment*, we mean *assessment for learning*, and, in particular, the teacher practices that help students learn how to learn. We mean to give students the tools to self-correct in order to be more successful in whatever task they encounter. We emphasize what *assessment for learning* looks like in practice.

What Are the Student Outcomes?

As a result of adopting new techniques to focus on the learner, teachers will find that student performance will improve and the students will see themselves as learners. More students will be successful in achieving the curricular outcomes as the teacher learns how to target their lessons and help the students identify problem areas in their own work.

In addition to being successful learners, students will understand how they came to learn. Students learn how to refine their thinking about what they can do successfully and what they will need to improve. By talking about themselves as learners, they develop and recognize repertoires of preferred strategies that work best for them. The assessment techniques not only result in more successful students but also give them the tools and reflective ability to learn independently of the teacher and to be lifelong learners.

We define a learner as someone who possesses three characteristics or skills:

- the ability to recognize what they know and what they can do
- the ability to identify what they are unsure of or have difficulty with
- the ability to identify the next steps he/she needs to take, or the strategies he/she uses to help solve problems

The Scaffolding Described

Primary students, from nursery school to grade 3, are not going to suddenly become active learners just because we want them to or because we encourage, plead, or beg. Unfortunately, there is no single thing that a teacher can do for young students to make them see themselves as successful learners. There is, however, a process that is relatively simple to understand, though not always easy to apply. We have broken the process into eight steps called the *scaffolding* (see figure 1.3).

Scaffolding

Setting the Target

Step 1 Understand the learning task and the learning intent.

Step 2 Share task/intent with students in accordance with the students' learning profile. Discuss, "What will it look like when we finish?"

Step 3 Design and carry out enabling tasks that lead students towards the learning goals.

Practice

Step 4 Provide a first attempt for the students to show what they know.

Step 5 Invite comparison.

Step 6 Have students identify the next step(s).

Step 7 Provide an opportunity for a second attempt to reach the goals, using the chosen next step.

Reflection

Step 8 Encourage the students to look back and reflect on themselves as learners.

Figure 1.3 Scaffolding for student learners.

We would like to give you a taste of what's to come in the rest of this book, and introduce you to how the scaffolding can be applied in a primary classroom. Let's look at a common primary classroom experience for students:

> The teacher calls all the students together to sit on the carpet so that he/she can start the day or explain a new activity. At this point, the teacher can begin the process of helping students to see themselves as learners. We use the scaffolding step called *Setting the Target*, with its three critical procedures (steps 1–3):

Step 1 Understand the learning task and the learning intent.

Step 2 Share task/intent with students in accordance with the students' learning profile. Discuss, "What will it look like when we finish?"

Step 3 Design and carry out enabling tasks that lead students towards the learning goals.

Before the lesson begins, the teacher must consider the intent of the lesson. Most teachers are very successful at describing a task to students, but it is sometimes difficult to clarify for the students what they should be learning. The teacher must also consider, "What will be a good job?" The clearer the target for students, the more successful students will be.

With all the students sitting on the carpet around the teacher, some fidgeting, some distracted, and some eagerly attentive, the *task* and *intent* are shared with the students. The teacher can help the students become involved in the process of learning by asking them to help come up with a criteria list that explains what it means to be successful in a given task. Ask the students, "What will this look like when we finish?" A list, developed by the teacher, can be presented as a back-up or if some critical points have been missed by the class effort (see chapter 3 for specific examples).

After the lesson has been explained, the intent made clear, and the task understood, the students will move efficiently on to their work. The next section of the scaffolding, called *Practice*, has four separate steps and becomes important as the students start to work:

Step 4 Provide a first attempt for the students to show what they know.

Step 5 Invite comparison.

Step 6 Have students identify the next step(s).

Step 7 Provide an opportunity for a second attempt to reach the goals, using the chosen next step.

This is important for students to have the chance to practise being learners, so they can acquire the language and build the skills needed to be learners. It is key for students to have a chance to work, to try something, and possibly get stuck so they internalize the process of working through a task to successful completion. The teacher has two roles – one, as an observer, and the second, as a coach. The teacher steps back, observes the students, and asks, "Where are students successful?" and, "What gaps in their learning are obvious?" These observations form the basis of future lessons.

Of course, a teacher's time for observation is constantly interrupted by questions from anxious students. The conversations between the teacher and students, though, are critical in our model for helping students think about their work.

Teachers must treat the students who have questions as learners. The teacher's first job is to help students see and talk about where they have already had success in the task, and then where they are unsure what to do next. Then the teacher can try to lead the student to explore various ways of getting unstuck. Chapter 2 will help with making these conversations productive, and gives examples and suggestions for getting started. The more often the teacher repeats a conversation with students, the more successful the students will be when they are asked to talk about themselves as learners.

The final stage of the assessment for learning process, *Reflection*, has only one step:

> **Step 8** Encourage the students to look back and reflect on themselves as learners.

Using our example of primary students assembled around the teacher in a group on a carpet and then moving on to work on the task on their own, step 8 will come as students are asked to finish their work and get ready for their next activity.

We have noticed that this step, reflection, is nearly always omitted. At the end of the time allotted for the task, teachers are under pressure to prepare the students for the next activity on the timetable. Primary students need a great deal of direction and moving smoothly to the next task becomes a priority. It is, however, possible for teachers to train themselves to ask the students, "Who thought they did a good job?" and to follow up with, "Can you tell me why?" Students use the list of criteria they helped create before they started the task to help them describe what part of their work is successful. One learning cycle is now completed and the teacher and students can continue the process as outlined by the eight steps of the scaffolding.

With step 8, teachers can use carefully constructed questions to help students think more deeply about their learning, both right at the end of a task, and after some time has passed. Primary students do not always remember events from a few days ago, let alone a few weeks ago.

We hope that this brief explanation of the scaffolding gives you a sense of what follows in the next few chapters. We hope also that you are thinking, Hey, this just sounds like good teaching! If you are, then you're right. These ideas are not new. The ideas and suggestions in this text are based upon the ideas from a review of educational literature that looked for innovations in classroom practice that really made a difference in student performance (Black and Wiliam, 1998). The research identified the most effective ways teachers have helped their students improve over many years.

We are sure you will recognize that you are already doing many parts of the scaffolding. In our experience, it is not that teachers don't know what to do, but that teachers try to do too much. This book and the scaffolding we provide help answer one important question, "What is the best way teachers can help students be successful independent learners?"

Where Should Teachers Begin?

Teachers should not necessarily feel compelled to work on the steps in the order they are listed in the scaffolding. Each teacher will know best what they already understand about assessment, what they already do with their students, and the amount of change they are willing to undertake. We recommend teachers first read the book to find some aspect of assessment that they find most appealing. Since all of the ideas we present are based upon the scaffolding, teachers may wish to use the steps as the basis for decision making on assessment.

The scaffolding makes choosing a starting point easier by providing a framework to organize many assessment ideas and giving teachers some sense of the big picture of assessment in the classroom. The eight steps suggest how individual ideas about assessment practice may be related to each other and how each may build upon the other towards helping students become independent learners.

The scaffolding organizes the many ideas about assessment in much the same way as a general lesson. The lesson is given, the students work through the task, and there is a summary event at the end of the lesson. The scaffolding parallels these stages in three sections, the set-up, the practice, and the reflection. Each stage identifies key teacher behaviours in assessment that help students become independent learners. A teacher who is planning a lesson and wondering, "What can I do to help my students be independent?" can refer to the scaffolding at each lesson-planning stage to help decide which ideas to incorporate.

In our work with teachers, the scaffolding was the most helpful way to begin thinking about assessment practices. Teachers were able to look at a broad range of assessment ideas and select an area to work on that would be most meaningful to them. The scaffolding is specific enough to help, but does not restrict teachers to any particular assessment strategies. Teachers are encouraged to read through the steps in the scaffolding and then choose at which point to enter the process, based on their previous experience and current assessment practices. The following examples (figure 1.4) show a variety of things teachers did as they began to understand assessment for learning. More examples can be found in chapter 3.

Nursery/Kindergarten
The teacher made it a practice to explain to her students the learning objectives for each activity the students did. The teacher found that the students were more focused in their work and their products were of higher quality when they understood why they were doing them.

Kindergarten
The teacher asked the children to develop a list of criteria for the behaviours that are appropriate for the classroom. The intent of the list was to help all students have a happy, good-learning room.

Grade 1
The students were given a chart that listed the steps they would take to complete a journal page. The teacher went over each step and worked through one example with the class. If a few students showed her an incomplete journal page, she just pointed in the direction of the chart listing the steps, and the students could self-correct.

Grade 1
The students worked with the teacher to build criteria for correct behaviours and for academic work. Anonymous pieces of work were critiqued by the class to establish what a good piece of work looks like. The teacher created an *object chart* to exemplify the criteria. For example, if students were supposed to look at the speaker while they listened, a pair of eyeglasses was taped to the object chart.

Grade 2
Students were given a rubric for writing, including mechanics and content. Students used the rubric to compare a piece of writing they had done at the beginning of the year with one they had just completed.

Grades 3 and 4
For each math lesson, students were given a rubric on chart paper and the students would complete an activity that was based upon the lesson. At the end of their work, students completed a reflection sheet based upon the rubric.

Figure 1.4 Primary teachers using the scaffolding.

The ideas presented in the scaffolding will be daunting for some, but we would like to emphasize that this process takes time, and the activities here could keep you busy for several years. Our best advice is to start modestly and use the three-level rubric (see appendix 4) based upon the scaffolding to evaluate your progress in assessment at the end of a term or at the end of a year. Application of even just one of the scaffolding steps will result in students becoming independent learners.

How Quickly Should Teachers Proceed?

The rate of change in primary classrooms depends on the speed of learning of the students. Nursery school to grade 3 students can make extraordinary progress in their abilities to be reflective learners. Their success depends on how carefully the classroom teacher helps her students acquire the critical skills they need and then how often they are allowed to use these new skills. However quickly the teacher would like to move ahead, it is the needs and abilities of the students that are most important.

When teachers are trying to improve their assessment programs, they should not underestimate the impact the environment of their school has on the students. Schools are complex societies that succeed by the good will and hard work of everyone in the building. Even though teachers often work alone in their classrooms, there will be demands that naturally arise from being in the school environment: special guests, concerts, a variety of in-services, safety procedures that must be practised, and so on. Teachers often must temporarily set aside their work in assessment for learning, deal with the interruption, and then return to their original task. This is not easy to do, but being aware of the natural rhythm of the school may help teachers anticipate and even plan for the disruptions, thus minimizing their impact.

Teachers will almost certainly suffer from implementation fatigue. In the beginning, the newness of the ideas and approaches carries teachers along and they have a sense that progress is being made. After a few months, it often becomes more difficult to remember what was so exciting in the first place. The students are not making the progress you had hoped and none of the ideas seem to work out as successfully as you had first imagined.

Inevitably, the learning curve will flatten out and, in teaching, it is very easy to change direction and find something else that must be done. One way teachers can be more patient and more persistent is to try to see themselves as learners. Adult learners need choice, time to work with colleagues, support, and an acknowledgement that change will occur much more slowly than anyone would wish. Teachers will also need opportunities for discussion with trusted colleagues. Professional discussions with colleagues who are in parallel situations can help deepen everyone's comprehension of their work. Teachers need regular support from sympathetic administrators and consultants who can act as critical friends by listening carefully, exploring ideas, and asking probing questions. Finally, adult learners, including teachers, need enough time. They need time to complete the cycle of work, time to pause, and then time to reflect so that deeper understanding can develop. We hope that teachers allow themselves the privilege of going slowly, think critically about the work, modify the ideas presented here on the basis of their judgment, and look for broader applications.

Self-Review: Setting a Baseline

A significant problem for teachers is gauging their progress as they work on improving their assessment programs. It is difficult to sort out new understandings from ideas that teachers already believed when they began. We invite teachers to spend the time they need to review their current thinking about assessment before moving ahead in the process of change.

After thinking about and answering the questions in figure 1.5, teachers should add two dates beside the questions. The first date will remind teachers of their initial thinking about the questions and the second date is a promise to revisit the questions to think about next steps. Teachers should be generous with setting the second date so that they can proceed slowly but deliberately to improve their practice before they have to reflect again.

In the past, what have I done to provide feedback to my students?

_____

_____

_____ Date: _____ Date: _____

How have I involved my students in their learning?

_____

_____

_____ Date: _____ Date: _____

What examples do I have of adjusting my teaching as a result of the outcomes of my assessments?

_____

_____

_____ Date: _____ Date: _____

Figure 1.5 Questions to ask before starting the process of change.

Our Reflection

The ideas in this series arose from a three-year program to help teachers develop their assessment techniques so that student performance improved and students came to see themselves as learners. Another strong theme that developed was that teachers needed to be treated like learners themselves if we wanted the ideas to be sustained.

At the end of each chapter, you will find an essay on one of the four main ideas that guided us as we developed a program that respected the needs of adult choices. We assume that the principal audience of this book will be classroom teachers and so each essay is written with them in mind. We hope teachers will learn from our experience to enhance their own journeys as they deepen their understanding of the art of teaching. However, all educators can read these essays as they try to design programs that not only help students but meet the learning needs of the teachers in their schools.

Time: An Essay

We advise that before you begin too much work on your assessment practices, you should consider how much time might be involved. The length of time required to accomplish change depends upon the depth you want to achieve. If you simply want to try out a few ideas, your time commitment will be very brief. If, however, you want to develop a deep understanding of the ideas presented here and apply them in many aspects of your teaching, you must allow yourself much more time. The length of time involved in the process of change is often underestimated. Without a realistic sense of how much time and effort are required, you might become frustrated at your rate of change. We want to emphasize that this process is lengthy, yet is exceedingly rewarding in the end.

We understand that we are rarely allowed the luxury of time. It is very reasonable that the people who implement new programs want to see results as quickly as possible. Generally, when there is a new initiative in a school division, the amount of time allowed for implementation is shorter than anyone would like, and certainly shorter than needed to make the best of the change. The cost of training teachers is very high. Efficient introduction of ideas and quick implementation are very important criteria when programs are designed to introduce new ideas to teachers.

As a teacher, you have a responsibility to yourself as well as your students. You have many programs already in place and many obligations to fulfill in your classroom. One basic question you should consider at the beginning of this process is, "What are your present commitments?" You cannot simply add something new to your plate and suppose that you are going to carry on trouble-free and succeed. The burden inevitably becomes too much so that every time you add something to your workload, something suffers.

You have learned that to be successful in the classroom, you have to develop procedures to be a successful manager. The procedures are habits that you have developed over the years through trial and error. Most teachers are not even aware of many of their routines because they have become habit. The habits save you from having to reinvent the wheel all the time, but they also do not change easily. It will take more time to understand how to accommodate the new ideas in your classroom situation and adapt them to your own style. Adaptation requires thinking. The more time you have to think, the easier it will be to make the changes.

It is not unreasonable to give yourself three to five years to come to a true, deep understanding of any new idea. Consider the first year as a general introduction. You spend your time getting a good feel for what is involved. You learn the vocabulary and try out a few things. Often, one problem in the first year of change is that the best ideas usually come after you have already made plans for what you wanted to accomplish and have set up routines for your classroom. Working around what is already established will make it more difficult to implement change. As a result, even though you might strongly believe in the work, you might not have a great deal to show for your first year of change.

Even though we began the work on assessment as a three-year project, and we had made this clear, all the participants felt as though something was wrong at the end of the first year because there was very little evidence of change. Teachers enjoyed the conversations and felt engaged in the work we were doing. They tried a few things in their classrooms and were pleased with their work. Still, there was a feeling of disappointment. The general feeling was that there should be more to show for all the work they were doing. Always, the push is for results over understanding.

After a year of introduction, the second year always seems much easier. You will feel more confident with the ideas about the program. This year you will do it right! And this is generally what happens. In year two, many of the early questions have been answered, so implementation will seem easier.

You are learning and you can expect to encounter difficulties because there will be things you had not considered. It is all part of the process, but the errors tend to stand out more than what you did right. Even the best teacher will have ideas that didn't work, students they didn't reach, and ideas they didn't get to because they ran out of time, money, energy, or all three. It would be a mistake to assume you are going to master these ideas in two years.

In year three, your learning is at yet another stage. The lustre has worn off and the new idea is no longer fresh. You are beginning to realize that the new techniques are not the complete answer to teaching. Experience has turned activities into tools for helping students. In year three, you can refine your ideas and the worksheets to make them better fit the needs of your classes. You question whether it is really worth the effort to pursue this particular educational approach. You are better able to see the shortcomings of your approach and see the modifications you need to make. In the third year, you can look for ways to adapt the basic ideas to areas of your program. You are making the ideas your own as your understanding deepens.

Year three comes with its own special set of problems. Teachers tend to forget what they didn't know when they began so long ago and downplay the advances they have made. Even though you have made significant gains, your achievements may not be near your original goals.

This is the nature of change.

So give yourself time. It is time to go deeply into one idea, such as assessment practices that will help students become independent learners. As you go deeply into one idea, you will see threads of connections to other ideas. Mastery is a worthy goal and time is your friend.

2

STUDENT LEARNERS

To be reflective means to mentally wander through where you have been and to try to make some sense out of it.
— Costa and Kallick, 2000

Guiding Questions

1. In which other ways could you describe a learner?

2. What would be the benefits/drawbacks of making "self-esteem" your main teaching goal?

3. What is lost if you set "improving grades" or "meeting curricular outcomes" as the only goal for students?

4. How would our definition of a student learner help with school portfolios?

5. How much time should you set aside in your planning to allow for building the language of reflection in your students?

Key Ideas of Chapter Two

• the target of assessment for learning is to create independent student learners

• questions should lead students to think about how they learn

• students need to know the language of reflection

Introduction

We will begin talking about the scaffolding by looking closely at the last step, reflection. While steps 1 though 7 should be seen as building towards teachers' success in this final step, true independence is achieved in the reflection process. This chapter is about helping teachers form a clear picture of what a student learner might look like at the end of the process of change. It is a fundamental principle of learning that the clearer the target, the greater the likely success in hitting the target.

In terms of the scaffolding (see figure 1.3) this target, reflection, is step 8:

Step 8 Encourage the students to look back and reflect on themselves as learners.

Steps 1–7 are designed to help the students become independent learners. Teachers will probably order their teaching following the sequence of the steps, but each part of the process will be made easier when they have a clear understanding of the goal.

Teachers may question the ability of their very young students to reflect on themselves as learners. Reflection is often considered a higher level thinking skill and is discussed in terms of the synthesis and evaluation of ideas. It is much less intimidating to think about the reflection chapter as "wandering" through experience.

If reflection is a journey through experiences, then it is the teacher's job to help the students be successful in their wandering by giving them specific guideposts. Teachers know that primary students are capable of wonderful achievements when material is presented in manageable steps and students are given many opportunities to practise their new skills. The intent of this book is to identify for teachers the steps they must take to help students be successful in reflecting on their learning experiences.

Teachers may also be reassured by the many examples in this text of primary students' careful thinking about the learning process as a result of teachers' assessment programs.

Definition of a Student Learner

Let's begin with defining what we mean by a *student learner*. Any student who has shown mastery of the curriculum content can be considered a learner. We take this definition one step further and suggest that a true learner is a student who both masters the content and also understands how he/she has come to learn.

A student often learns a task or skill without thinking about how it all happened. We envision students being able to carry forward their knowledge of how they learned so that they are better prepared for the new learning experiences they will encounter in subsequent grades. Our main goal is to help students be successful in learning the curricula outcomes and be able to articulate how they came to be successful.

Our definition identifies three key behaviours of student learners:

1. **Possess the ability to recognize what they know or what they can do.** Students must be able to recognize in themselves that they can and have learned. They must be able to see and recognize that they can do some things well. The first part of the definition of a learner is particularly important for students who have had little success in school. Weaker students wrongly believe that they cannot do anything well and that if they were smart, then learning would be automatic. The teacher's job is to draw the student's attention to their specific strengths and to do this as often as possible.

2. **Possess the ability to identify what they are unsure of, or have difficulty with.** Student learners recognize that it is normal to get stuck while working on a task. They accept that they will encounter problems and some things will not have an immediate answer. They know that if they persevere, they will find a way to solve their problem and move on. Students who do not see themselves as learners tend to see problems as a whole. They either get it or they don't. They do not know how to break their problems down into smaller, more manageable, parts. Teachers can help students refine their thinking about problems by reviewing key aspects of the task and intents with students (see step 1 of the scaffolding).

3. **Possess the ability to identify their next steps or have strategies to help them with their difficulties.** Successful students are capable of identifying parts of their work that have to be improved. Successful students also have a variety of ways to help themselves when they come up against problems. Less successful students need to be taught the skills of reviewing their work critically and need help to build repertoires of problem-solving strategies.

An example of a student learner

Natasha was a grade 2 student who had difficulty reading. After some weeks of extra help with her reading skills, Natasha was asked to reflect on her experience and tell what she had learned (see figure 2.1).

Natasha's experience shows what is achievable for all struggling students with the patient application of best assessment practices. We see that Natasha is a learner as we have defined it. She knows her strengths, and the areas she has difficulty with, and can find a strategy to help her when she gets stuck. Natasha is very specific. She says, "Now I read long books. I can (write) more (words) and read more books. I can do my work (faster)...." Natasha can also name several very specific strategies. She says, "I (learned) how to (sound words). I go back and read to find what that (word) is. I read on to find what that (word) is."

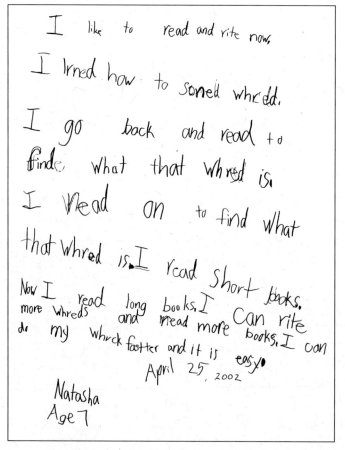

Figure 2.1 Natasha's reflections on her learning.

What Helps Teachers?

In the first two years of working with teachers, we discovered that most were not asking their students to reflect on themselves as learners. We had encouraged teachers to choose where they wanted to begin on the scaffolding, and most had chosen to concentrate on the first seven steps. They had seen great progress in their students' performance, but they usually did not ask their students to explicitly talk or write about themselves as learners (step 8). Often, the teachers couldn't understand why they had not followed through to step 8, even though they knew the students' ability to talk about their learning was important.

There is a practical reason why teachers find it difficult to ask students to reflect on themselves as learners. This reason mostly has to do with lack of time. Reflection most often comes near the end of units and endings are almost always frantic in any classroom. The end of a teaching period always seems to come up much more quickly than teachers expect and there is a rush just to get everything done on time.

We suggest ways to help teachers get through the hubbub at the end of a unit and include reflection as a key part of creating student learners.

Begin at the planning stage

To help teachers with the end of their units, we suggest looking closely at the beginning of the content unit. While planning a new lesson or unit, we suggest adding one more outcome: "Students will be able to talk about how they came to learn." Adding this statement will help teachers give priority to talking about learning in the day-to-day activities of a busy classroom. The teacher attends to the question, "Are they learning?" and at the same time continually asks, "Are they thinking and talking about learning?"

Planning from the beginning of a unit benefits the teacher because reflection is incorporated as a timed item in the lesson/unit plan. The students benefit because they are told early in the unit that one important expectation of the activity is their ability to reflect upon themselves as learners at the end. At the beginning of the lesson/unit, the students are told that not only will they be asked to show their understanding of the outcomes, but they must also be able to talk about how they learned, what gave them problems, and how they helped themselves when they didn't understand something. In figure 2.2 we suggest a framework that teachers can use to help explain to their students that they will be asked to think about how they came to learn.

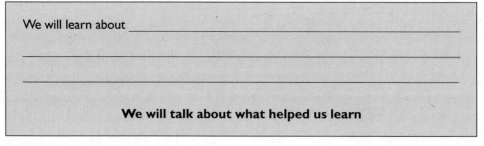

| We will learn about _____ |
| _____ |
| _____ |
| **We will talk about what helped us learn** |

Figure 2.2 Informing the students of expectations.

Describe the target

Once the teacher has decided that the students will have to be able to talk about how they learned, the next step is to make this goal clear to the students. One method is to turn the list of characteristics of a learner into a series of questions. In our definition of a learner, the first characteristic is that the learner must know what they can do. This might become the question, "What are you good at?" Similarly, the second characteristic of a learner, someone who can identify what they have difficulty with, might be, "What do you find most difficult?" And a third question for the last characteristic – can identify next steps or has strategies to help – might be, "What strategies do you use when you are stuck?"

Introducing the questions can be done after the class has finished a lesson and project. The whole class can offer suggestions and the responses recorded on chart paper. The teacher may repeat this whole-class exercise several times before the questions are used as a guide to interview individual students. Older students may use the form independently to begin practising writing about their own learning preferences. Figure 2.3 is an example of a form that teachers might use to record student interviews or for students who have enough writing skills to use independently.

In these sample questions, we have used the word *strategy*, which will probably be a new vocabulary word for primary students. This does not mean that it is too difficult for very young students to understand. Young students are very quick to learn new words and will start using the word easily. *Strategy* is a great word for teachers and students to start using as early as possible. As the teacher begins to use the term more often in their teaching, students begin to see that, when the teacher asks them to do something, it is because it will help them learn. Students start to see how activities such as finger counting in math or making a chart can help them learn math.

Reflecting as a Learner

Name: _____   Date: _____

Grade: _____   Subject/Unit: _____

Think back on the work we have done over the past little while.

What are you good at? _____

_____

What do you find most difficult?_____

_____

What strategies do you like to use when you are stuck or having difficulties?_____

_____

Figure 2.3 Questions to guide reflection.

After some time, teachers can use the questions on reflection to review their students' progress and decide if the students are ready to move on to the next steps. Once students have demonstrated their basic understanding of the questions, they need help from the teacher to think more carefully about their responses.

There are a number of other ways that teachers can help their students reflect on their learning. For example, students can share their answers with the whole class and the feedback or comments from the others will help them expand their thinking. The quality of responses to the questions on the forms will improve as the class has more opportunities to think about and discuss these questions. Teachers can also add other questions that will help extend and deepen a student's thinking about how they learn best. Interviewing the students to give deeper understanding is often a good idea.

Questions for quality

Figure 2.4 lists some suggested questions designed to help move students' thinking beyond superficial levels. Teachers may use these questions as a guideline to help them formulate their own set of questions to ask their students in interviews.

1. In your work on _____(making graphs, counting), what do you think you did well? How do you know?

2. What did you find most difficult? Can you tell me about it?

3. What did you do to solve the difficulty, to help you get beyond the problem? What was that like?

4. Tell me as many other ways that you know of that you might have used to get out of this difficulty, besides asking your friends or asking the teacher. (Continue until the student has reached his/her limit.)

5. From your list of strategies, which is your favourite? Why is it your favourite?

6. What are the problems in using this strategy?

7. Can you describe a situation outside school where you might use this same strategy?

Figure 2.4 Interview questions to deepen student understanding.

The first three questions reflect the definition of a learner. Each question has a *tag question* (see underlined question below) that is meant to prompt the student to think in some detail of their learning experience. The tag question helps make the student's thinking more precise.

1. In your work on _____ (making graphs, counting), what do you think you did well? How do you know?

2. What did you find most difficult? Can you tell me about it?

3. What did you do to solve the difficulty, to help you get beyond the problem? What was that like?

The following three questions focus on developing the students' abilities to solve their own problems. The questions challenge the student to name as many alternate strategies as possible.

4. Tell me as many other ways that you know of that you might have used to get out of this difficulty, besides asking your friends or asking the teacher. (Continue until the student has reached his/her limit.)

The goal of asking students to think hard about their learning is to make sure they consider their alternatives beyond the two most commonplace strategies to this question – asking a friend, or asking the teacher. While these are valid strategies, we want students to try more complex and independent strategies. The full potential of question 4 hinges on how successfully the teacher can push his/her students to think deeply. We recommend approaching this question lightheartedly in the interview and repeating, "What else?" in an exaggerated tone after the student reveals each of his/her strategies. This way, it becomes a game for the student as they try to name as many strategies as possible. This also helps develop a student's flexibility and encourages him/her to think about multiple ways of solving problems.

5. From your list of strategies, which is your favourite? Why is it your favourite?

In this question, students are asked to choose a favourite strategy. This forces them to develop a sense of personal preference and learning style. Students need to understand that one strategy may work well for some, but it will not necessarily work well for them. Students who are visual learners may like to make sketches to help their thinking, while others prefer to make lists of ideas. Answering the question helps students be more aware of the strategies they use automatically and without really thinking about why they work one way or another.

6. What are the problems in using this strategy?

Students need to learn to be critical thinkers about how they learn. This question suggests that there are good and bad aspects to any thinking strategy they choose. Students are learning that they should always look for two sides of an issue.

7. Can you describe a situation outside school where you might use this same strategy?

The final question encourages students to think beyond the classroom and about how they might apply their knowledge in other situations. This question demands a higher level of thinking and the student will need some time to think it through.

Teachers must use their best judgment of their students' readiness when deciding the exact wording of the interview questions. Teachers should add, delete, or reword the questions to best suit the needs of their particular class. Below, you will see three variations of questions (see figures 2.5, 2.6, 2.7) teachers have used to reach the students in their classes.

1) What is going well? What is the easiest part?

> making the questions. because there are some on the chart already.

2) What is the most difficult part(s)?

> finding the solutions to the question.

3) What strategies are you using?

> Think about what learned before and how you can use it

4) Why did you choose the strategy (or strategies)?

> I chose it because today earlier we were taking about recycling and it is easy to remember.

5) What other strategies might you have used?

> skip the difficult ones then go back to them.

Figure 2.5 Example of interview questions. *Lyn Peterson, Pat Deluca, grades 3–4.*

Topic: Sorting + Classifying

Write about a time during this project that you weren't sure what to do next - you got STUCK.

> I got stuck when I was sorting and got something that didn't fit in my other catagory

How did you help yourself to fix the problem?

> I made an other catagory so I could put my object in.

Figure 2.6 Example of interview questions. *Lyn Peterson, Pat Deluca, grades 3–4.*

```
┌─────────────────────────────────────────────────────────────────┐
│                           DURING                                  │
│                                                                   │
│     Name: _____                      │
│     Date:  _____                                               │
│     Grade: _____                                               │
│     Task/Unit: _____                     │
│                                                                   │
│     1) What is the best part of your work?                       │
│                                                                   │
│     2) What is not as good as you wish?                          │
│                                                                   │
│     3) What did you use to help you make things easy?            │
│                                                                   │
│     4) What strategies could you use to help you with the difficult part(s)? │
│                                                                   │
│     5) What else could you do?                                    │
│                                                                   │
└─────────────────────────────────────────────────────────────────┘
```

Figure 2.7 Example of interview questions. *Lidi Kuiper, grades 3, 4, 5, art.*

In the above sample questionnaires, you will notice that teachers have deleted some of the original questions from figure 2.4, and have reworded others to be more effective with their students. All three questionnaires have the same intent: deepening students' understanding of themselves as learners.

Expand one-word responses

When some students are asked about their learning, they can manage limited one- or two-word answers. And, when pressed by the teacher, these students turn their eyes downward and are silent. Even the most experienced teachers will have trouble coaxing longer responses from these students. If there are only one or two students in this situation, the teacher can call on the rest of the class to model longer answers. The problem may diminish over time as the taciturn students listen as their classmates respond. Listening to how other students respond helps the quiet students form their thoughts and find words to express themselves. Shy students will benefit from working in groups or with a partner who will help them become used to conversations about learning.

When the majority of students give only limited answers, the situation changes for the teacher. If the class as a whole is reluctant to give responses and there are no models or examples for the teacher to share with students, the problem gets worse and students find it difficult to reflect on their learning.

One approach is for teachers to look at the situation as a vocabulary or language learning issue. In the same way that students need help with new vocabulary in math and science before they can be successful, students may need direct instruction with the vocabulary and phrases they will need in order to talk about themselves as learners. Teachers have to ask themselves: "What questions will I ask my students about their learning?" and "What would be the appropriate responses?" The essential language associated with answering these questions is shared with the students and posted so that they have something to which they can refer. The language chart is explained to students and then practised many times. As a result of this very controlled practice, teachers will find that students begin to give more complex responses to questions about their learning.

We have included the experience of a grade 3 teacher who used language to help her students expand their ability to talk about their learning.

The teacher found that even by December, only a few students could respond to questions with answers of more than a few words each, and most of the time, when asked a question, her students were silent. The next science unit would require students to give explanations and the teacher realized that her students would need support to talk about their work.

The science unit was designed to help students understand the relationship between living things and soil. As part of the unit, students studied several types of soil in hands-on experiments and learned that different soil types had different characteristics. To conclude the unit, students were required to choose the most appropriate soil for different tasks and then explain their choices.

The teacher decided which questions she would use to prompt student explanations and the phrases the students would need to help them start their answers. The question and language prompts were made into a poster (see figure 2.8) and reviewed with the students.

The wall chart helps the students understand that there are different kinds of responses, some better than others. To challenge students to give longer, more complex answers, each response was shown as a different level of success. The teacher added picture symbols, related to the unit of study, which reflected the different levels of quality for each type of answer. An answer of "I don't know" was at the first level and was represented as the unopened flower. The last category is represented by a variety of flowering plants, indicating an answer addressing several aspects of a student's choice. At each level, the teacher has provided phrases that helped the students get started.

With the language chart in place, the students carried out a variety of experiments about soils. Once the investigations were completed, students were given tasks that required them to apply their knowledge of soils. In the first task, students were asked to imagine that they were a plant and they had to tell what soil they would choose to grow in, and why. After the task was completed, each student was interviewed and asked by the teacher to explain their answers.

Figure 2.8 Grade 3 wall chart sample with levels of responses. *Kim Wade.*

The students were asked to consider the wall chart titled "How Did You Get that Answer?" before conferencing with me. Although some students were still unable to verbally explain their thinking, ... I was pleased to hear some students reminding others, "Don't say, 'I don't know!'"

— Kim Wade, grade 3

Although the students had made some progress in their ability to explain their answers, the teacher was convinced they could do better. She gave the students a second task. In this task, the students were given live butterfly cocoons and were told that when the cocoons opened, the emerging butterflies would need grass to eat. The students were given grass seed, but the students had to choose the correct soil for the grass seed to sprout in time for the emergence of the butterfly. The question the students had to answer was, "What soil will you choose?" The students worked enthusiastically and took the task very seriously. Everyone was thrilled when their butterflies emerged and the grass had grown and was ready for the insects to eat.

In this case, the teacher interviewed the students twice; once, when the grass was just starting to grow and then again after the students could see they had successfully grown the grass. The teacher asked, "What was your answer to the question about what soil to choose?" and then, referring to the chart, "How did you get that answer?"

The student responses became longer and more specific with the second question. Not only did students show they understood the basic science, but they also showed they had a specific awareness of their knowledge, and they had the language to express their thinking. For example, here are some student comments about growing grass successfully:

- Water will get to the roots faster, I know because of the funnel experiment.
- Sand grew the bean in the bag and in the cup. Soil would have more nutrients for plants.
- Humus on top, and sand on the bottom because sand will suck up all the water and humus is healthy for the plant.
- I used everything. Soil is best to give lots of food. Worms are needed for air holes. Rocks and sand will help to hold it in the ground and hold water. I know this from the experiments we did, especially from planting beans.

Students who had earlier been willing only to give very short answers were now capable of practising much longer responses. The teacher helped them by indicating the key questions, words, and phrases they would need to help them respond. After several chances to practise, the students succeeded in expressing how they understood their learning.

Choice: An Essay

In our conversations with teachers, we realized that teachers wanted help finding places to begin and help getting over the emotional impact that accompanies each new request to change.

Adult learners must find ways to choose their own entry point, but some choices offered to teachers are too broad. Most in-services given to teachers contain too many ideas. In most respects, in-services are usually very positive events. You see colleagues you haven't spoken to in a long time, and the presenters are energetic, talented people with packets of good ideas. At the end of the day of in-service you feel pumped, ready to go back into the classroom, recharged with enthusiasm with a surfeit of ideas from which to choose. The next day the packets of ideas are placed in a filing cabinet or a box, or on a shelf, never to be opened. An idea or a strategy may be wonderful in the abstract but you have to make it fit into your already busy program. To fit the new idea or strategy into your program, you need a level of understanding that is not always possible to achieve in a one-day introduction. Too many ideas do not help teachers make choices.

Our first in-services followed this pattern. We had distributed excellent resources and teachers came away from the day feeling very positive. The ideas were research-based and were presented clearly in an engaging manner, but they were too broad for teachers to absorb in one day.

The scaffolding was used to give teachers more manageable choices. The scaffolding was broad enough to give teachers a general understanding of the big picture of assessment practices after one or two opportunities to review it. It was specific enough so that teachers could recognize some elements of their own teaching. Teachers chose points of entry based upon how they could most easily adapt or modify what they were already doing.

The choices presented to teachers can be too narrow. Supposing a principal approaches a teacher and asks, "Would you like to participate in ...?" Is this a choice? Can a teacher say "No" to the principal? Many teachers feel it would be unwise to decline. Some feel they will lose their job or a transfer will be blocked, or their evaluation is this year, or they want to seem like team players. All these anxieties, largely imagined, prevent teachers from seeing the question as an opportunity.

Administrators we worked with were surprised when we shared this point of view. When we began our program, we had asked the principals to recruit only interested participants from their schools. In a few instances the principals approached teachers directly. In good faith, they genuinely believed they were giving teachers a choice when they asked them if they would like to participate. The administrators only asked because they respected the teacher and believed the opportunity would benefit the teacher. It is an unfortunate dynamic that teachers feel they have to second-guess their administrators. The net result is that teachers feel they have little choice when asked by an administrator to participate.

Over the course of your career, you will be introduced to many new programs. However, only in the rarest of circumstances will you be asked if you want or need the program. They will just arrive. The problem is further compounded by the number of such programs that come at you like waves on a beach. All of them will have educational value and all of them will be introduced with the purpose of improving the educational experiences of your students. As a professional, serious about your responsibility of educating young people, you might be forgiven for being resentful. On the one hand, you are told to be responsible for your classroom, and then, on the other, it seems as though you are being told you are not responsible – do it this way. In our work we tried to avoid this scenario by asking schools to volunteer to work in the program. In the first year, 4 out of 21 schools chose to participate and, in the second year, 6 more schools were ready to take part.

New programs are introduced on the basis of "rational" premises. The educational ideas are sound and, therefore, it is reasonable that teachers should want to improve their teaching in this way. Rationally, the ideas make sense. But, from everything we have learned about the brain, we know there are no purely rational ideas. All ideas have an emotional component that may prompt an adverse reaction.

Even if your classroom practices are not up to the latest research findings, you value them because you have put a great deal of effort into making them work. You may feel that the new program devalues your sincere effort to do a good job. You may also feel that you are being asked to add another task to your already overburdened schedule. However you may feel about being put in this position, it is left to you to manage this emotional impact. Reminding yourself that this is a normal reaction will help somewhat. You may also remind yourself that you are part of a large, complex system in which decisions must be made and that it is impossible to consult each teacher individually beforehand. Share your frustrations with trusted colleagues. It is not complaining; it is dealing with an honest reaction. Much of our time as support people to teachers was spent in listening sympathetically to teachers share their anxieties about their work. These feelings had to be expressed and honoured before any progress could be made.

When you feel you are ready, look for choices that are available to you. You may not be able to accept all the ideas presented at first, but undoubtedly you will be able to find something. As you look through your options, distinguish between what you must do and what you will choose to learn in some depth. As a teacher, you have developed an instinct for what will help students. Use this experience to guide your decisions about those aspects in which you are genuinely interested. Search out ideas that will help your students be more successful and your job easier. What you choose to learn may seem small at first, relative to what you are asked to do, but eventually it will have far greater impact than if you didn't make a choice. Choose from a position of strength, based upon what you already know. Choose an area in which you feel you still have room to develop. Choose something knowing you won't get it exactly right the first time but you will be willing to persist and adapt as needed. You will come to a deeper understanding of the issues involved and your teaching will become stronger.

Not only can you control what particular aspect you are going to work on in depth, you can also choose the rate at which you deepen your understanding. Your progress in any one area will be affected by your range of commitments. If your responsibilities extend over many tasks, then, of course, you must lower your expectations in any one topic. Slow it down, go carefully.

As support persons, it was our job to convince the teachers that our work wasn't just about "doing something"; we were asking teachers to "rethink" their practice. In our conversations we would ask them to talk about what they were already doing in assessment and help them to see parallels to what was outlined in the scaffolding. These conversations clarified and strengthened the ways in which they were already helping their students become independent learners. With this approach, almost all the teachers we worked with were able to choose an area they felt would benefit their programs.

You can practise this process using this book. We invite you to read over this book and choose a point of entry. What strikes a chord of familiarity? Congratulate yourself for what you are already doing to make students independent learners. Do you want to spend more time developing what you are working on now? How might you adapt a particular idea to your work? No matter where you start, as you dig deeply into any one area, you will find the one idea that will eventually lead you to all the other ideas in this book.

Choose to be a learner with your students.

3

CLEAR TARGETS

What is needed is a culture of success, backed by a belief that all pupils can achieve.

– Black and Wiliam, 1998

Guiding Questions

1. Do students always have to know the intent of a task?

2. Do students who can't read benefit from the intent being written out?

3. When is the best time during a lesson to introduce the task and intent to primary students?

4. What images/symbols can be associated with each criterion?

Key Ideas of Chapter Three

- students need to know "why"

- task and intent should be posted

- students should help define the criteria for success

- the Task/Intent/Criteria model increases student performance

Introduction

In chapter 2, we discussed the goal of assessment for learning as developing student learners. We emphasized our definition of a student learner and the design of appropriate questions for students, based upon the definition. Teachers are now ready to begin planning their daily assessment, which will support their defined assessment goals. It is very straightforward. Good assessment begins with setting clear targets.

Students need daily success to build the confidence to answer the end-of-term question, "What are you good at?" The frequency of student success increases when teachers set clear learning targets. Clear targets help students identify what they have done well and make it easier for students to solve their problems. In this chapter, we will outline some of the key points for setting targets that will help students succeed.

Steps 1–3 of the scaffolding have a special poignancy for students in nursery school to grade 3. The success, or lack of success, is critical in a student's formative years and influences all their future school experiences. Not only do students have to acquire the fundamentals of reading and writing in these early years, but they must also develop the confidence that they can learn.

The scaffolding (see figure 1.3) breaks the task of developing targets into three distinct steps.

Setting the Target

Step 1 Understand the learning task and the learning intent.

Step 2 Share task/intent with students in accordance with the students' learning profile. Discuss, "What will it look like when we finish?"

Step 3 Design and carry out enabling tasks that lead students towards their learning goals.

The teacher plays the central role in directing learning by setting the targets, but as the teacher and students work through each step, more of the responsibility for learning is transferred to the students. The teacher takes responsibility for deciding what the students will do and what will be learned from the activity. The teacher then begins to share the responsibility for the learning with the students by describing the task and what is to be learned, then inviting the students to help describe how they will know they have done a good job. The teacher's short lesson is focused on providing the vocabulary and skills that students need in order to work independently of the teacher.

The Three Steps

The following step-by-step discussion shows how each step helps clarify the learning targets for students. Defining the task, intent, and criteria (TICs) in the first three steps is a key activity, and we recommend that they be recorded on wall charts, or TIC charts. We have illustrated each step with examples from teachers and students from nursery school to grade 3 to show the importance of each step in helping students reach our overall goal of becoming independent student learners.

Step 1: Understand the learning task and the learning intent

This step can be deceptive. It seems straightforward, but even very experienced teachers may pay attention only to the task and ignore the intent. The *intent* is a statement of the learning that must occur as a result of the activity. The intent labels the centre of teachers' lessons and helps teachers decide what must be stressed. Only when the teachers have fixed the intent in their own mind will they be able to make the intent clear to students.

The first priority for most teachers is to identify the activities and think about how to explain them to the students. Often, only a small amount of time is spent thinking about why the activity is needed in the first place. A basic understanding of teaching young students is that they must always be doing something in order to learn. Students at this early stage of their schooling do not like to just sit, they want to be active. Teachers know this and spend a great deal of their time carefully organizing active-learning activities for their young students.

Even if the curriculum documents suggest appropriate activities, there is still a great deal of planning and preparation work for teachers to do. What materials will be needed? Is there a best sequence for the activity? What is the best order? How much time will be needed? Which students will need special attention? Teachers get caught up in the logistics of the activity and, as a consequence, consideration of the intent of the activity is often set aside.

Many times teachers have favourite activities that they repeat from year to year. Teachers sense that the students are learning from watching them engage in activities and the quality of the finished products they see. Teachers assume that the intent is not important to the students. However, we have found that identifying the intent helps move the lesson from the general to the more specific.

The importance of step 1 is in how it helps teachers present their lessons as learning events rather than simply as busy activities. Thinking about the intent helps teachers narrow the scope of the lesson and focus on what is truly important. It takes practise to identify the intent of a lesson. The first few tries will take more time, but once teachers develop a new way of thinking about their lessons, it becomes easier to identify their intents.

In the following examples of task and intent, we have described four lessons taken from teachers with whom we worked. We describe the task that the teacher gave to students and we invite you to think about what you would choose as the intent of the lesson if they were your lessons. After thinking about your choice, compare it with the intent of the teachers in our examples.

What would you consider to be the intent in the following examples?

Situation 1: Phys. Ed. Grades 1–3

In the grade 1–3 classes we worked on galloping. The task "galloping" was written on chart paper. We discussed why we were learning to gallop.
We are learning to gallop because_____.

Galloping criteria were written on chart paper. We'll know we know how to gallop because:

1. One foot will lead and the other will be brought rapidly up to it

2. Knees are bent

3. Flight is low

4. Hips and shoulders face the direction of movement

5. Body is relaxed

6. Galloping is rhythmical

The students are learners. How else would you teach galloping without giving students the criteria? It only makes sense that you would tell students why they are learning something.

– J. Hancharyk, physical education

Situation 2: Sharing Time Nursery/Kindergarten

... at circle time, good listening and looking was defined as: no hands or feet, kind words, wait until you hear your name before answering a question, and so on. Then it was more personalized to what it is you need to work on to earn the award. The shared task/intent is _____.

– Lucy Carter, grade N/K

Situation 3: Sharing Time Nursery/Kindergarten

I was frustrated that students were continually coming to me or the teacher aides to get help with their spelling, even though the students had spent a great deal of time learning many other strategies for checking the spelling of words. I then explained to the students (and to the teacher aide) that the intent of having all the strategies was to _____.

I posted a chart that had a list of five options that students could use when they become stuck:

1. Word Wall

2. Dictionary

3. Look around the room

4. Sound it out

5. Ask an adult

Students were told how each option would work. Each was demonstrated. They practised each and were told to try one or all before asking for help.

It worked with varying levels of independence. Students have begun to use their favourite strategies before asking for help. Struggling students will practise the routine of these ideas with assistance from an adult.

– Rhett Turner, grade 2/3

Situation 4: Writing Process Grade 2

I had the grade 2 class assess the writing process after a writing project on the First Nation Peoples.

We discussed that there would be four main parts to the writing process and that we would examine each one separately as we worked through the project. I explained that an author follows the same steps and gave many examples.

Before/after each part of the writing process we brainstormed steps. The intent given to the children was _____.
It was a slow process but very powerful and productive. The whole process took about a month.

– Patricia Deluca, grade 2

Actual intent for situation #1
Movement skills will help us in sports when we get to upper grades.

Actual intent for situation #2
The shared task/intent is to have a happy, "good-learning" room for all 32 of us (it is pointed out this requires all our cooperation/good-classroom behaviour).

Actual intent for situation #3
I then explained to the students (and to the teacher aide) that the intent of having all the strategies was so that they did not have to go to an adult for help.

Actual intent for situation #4
The intent given to the students was, "What we were going to do/what we had done/what our next steps would be."

After reading through the examples, teachers may find that the intent they chose was different from the intent of teachers in each situation. Differences in intents are to be expected because activities or lessons may have several possible intents. Teachers must choose the most appropriate intent for their students. Whatever intent they choose, it narrows the focus so they can be more efficient and students can have a better chance of understanding what they are expected to learn.

We suggest that teachers work with their colleagues to find the intent of any lesson at the beginning of the lesson-planning stage. Working with others helps expand the thinking behind the intent of a lesson, and will likely bring out new ideas. Remembering to ask, "Why are we teaching this?" will make it easier to define the intent of any lesson. Often, the question will be met with silence, as each teacher in the group thinks carefully about the intent. Ideas slowly emerge and are then refined. We recommend that one person be designated as the notetaker, collecting the answers on a piece of chart paper as the group talks.

The diagram in figure 3.1 may help organize your thoughts about the task and intent of your lesson. While you may not choose to fill in all the boxes, the answers to any of the questions can help define your intent. If you use the diagram to determine the intent of a variety of lessons, you may find some questions better than the others for different subject areas. Distribute the form to your colleagues as you try to define the intent of your lesson and use the group's feedback to help you. Look at the kinds of ideas each person suggested and work together to clarify the intent of each.

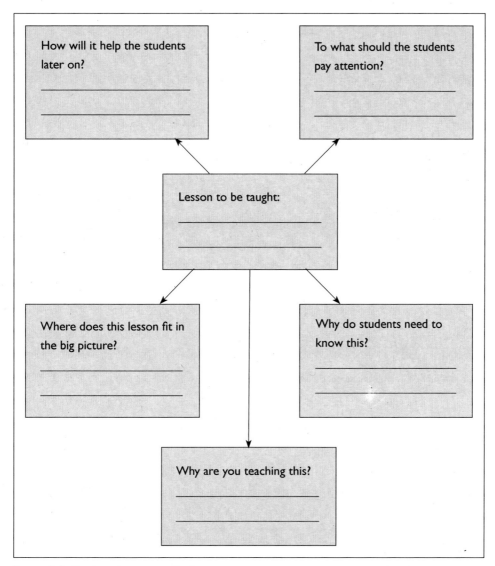

Figure 3.1 Finding the intent of a lesson.

Step 2: Share task/intent with the students in accordance with the students' learning profiles. Discuss, "What will it look like when we finish?"

In step 1, teachers spend time thinking about what they want students to learn, the intent, and how the learning will be achieved, the task. In step 2, teachers help students understand what they will be doing and what they have to learn.

Step 2 has two main parts:
- sharing the task/intent with students
- helping students develop a sense of ownership for their learning

Teaching a lesson to students in nursery school to grade 3 requires a special skill. The instructions must be presented clearly and each new term should be carefully explained. Teachers must pay attention to the pace of the lesson and be prepared for minds that tend to wander off topic. Even in the early years, students all learn in different ways.

We use the term *students' learning profile* to capture the variety of ways that students absorb information and how they choose to express their ideas. The discussions about receiving and giving information to students have been labelled many different ways (e.g., learning styles, learning modalities, multiple intelligences, and so on). Teachers know that when they share information with their students, they have to do so in a variety of ways if they want to reach every type of learner. They may communicate verbally, in writing, by using symbols or images, kinaesthetically, or some combination of these tools.

> Clarke's (1998) *Targeting Assessment in the Primary Classroom* is filled with examples of teachers sharing the task/intent with their students. The reported results are astounding and we recommend taking a look.

Grades N–3 teachers know the importance of using language that is at the appropriate level and tend to focus on giving very clear verbal instructions. It is important to explain clearly because of the differences in learning profiles. More students will understand the task and intent if the explanation includes key words that are written out and symbols are added next to the written descriptions (see figure 3.2). Students may also demonstrate the main points of the lesson for each other, e.g., how to use manipulatives in math, good group-work behaviour, or walking over to the Word Wall to find the correct spelling of a word.

Figure 3.2 Grade 2 example of poster with guidelines for editing marks.

The quality of students' performance increases when they have a sense of ownership for their work. Teachers can encourage ownership by asking students to think about the finished products before they begin. Once the teacher has explained the task and intent, the teacher should ask the students, "What will a good job look like?"

Posing this question helps the students see the assignment in their own terms. Students bring their past experiences to the new assignment and this deepens their understanding of what they must do. The student suggestions, along with the teacher's contributions, become a list of criteria that students can use to guide their work and to decide if they have done a good job.

The criteria for a well-done assignment should be written out, along with a brief description of the task and intent. Teachers should be careful about the number of criteria for success introduced at one time. Over time, teachers can build quite a long and complicated list of criteria for students. When the majority of students have mastered the skills in the list of criteria, teachers may consider adding to the list. Remember, listing criteria with the help of students will take more time in the beginning, but will go more quickly with more practise.

If time is of greater importance, make the lesson move more quickly by listing the criteria without involving the students. The advantage is that it seems to save time at the beginning of the lesson. The criteria can be reviewed quickly in class time, and the students can begin working sooner. We have found that the disadvantage is that the students may actually take longer to complete the work. Teacher-created criteria lists may be beyond the student's understanding. The teacher may not realize that the students are struggling to understand until they are in the middle of their work and become frustrated with making mistakes. As the gaps in student understanding begin to appear, the teacher may have to stop the class and reteach parts to the lesson. Involving students in creating the list of criteria will help avoid any unnecessary classroom disruption.

If the students are aware of the task/intent/criteria (TICs), more students will succeed and more students will work independently of the teacher. Thinking and talking about the TICs clarify what is truly important for both the teacher and the students. Figure 3.3 offers a structure for recording the TICs in your classroom.

TIC Talk

Task ________________________________ "Do"

Intent ________________________________ "Think About"

Criteria ________________________________ "Look For"

____

____

____

Figure 3.3 TIC Talk: Recording the task, intent, and criteria of a lesson.

Teachers may hesitate to write out the TICs for students. A good place to start using the TIC format is with an activity that continues over several weeks. For example, journal writing is a commonly used activity that many teachers use to help students develop their writing skills. Figure 3.4 is an example of the criteria list for journal writing that one teacher posted for grade 2 students. This list was developed with students over a period of time.

Teachers might also consider asking their teacher aide to write out the task and intent. Besides taking some of the burden from the teacher, the teacher aide's writing is a check on the clarity of the teacher's instructions. It also insures that the teacher aide and the teacher are on the same page.

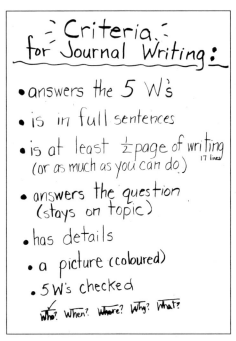

Figure 3.4 Example of seven journal-writing criteria for grade 2 students.

Step 3: Design and carry out enabling tasks that lead students toward the learning goal(s)

Our understanding of this step has changed since we first began working with teachers. We first believed that step 3 was simply about a teacher teaching the lesson, which was distinct from creating student learners. Preparing students to be learners occurred before the lesson in steps 1 and 2, and afterwards, by helping students to reflect on their work in steps 4–8. Originally, we had included step 3 so that teachers could see where to fit it in the lesson with the work of creating independent student learners. As we watched teachers work in the classroom and talked with them about their understanding of step 3, we refined our thinking.

> The term *enabling task*, originally coined by Wiggins and McTighe (2005), stresses the connection between a learning activity and the learning goals.

We now understand that step 3 is part of setting the target for students. Step 3 is about the *how* to complete the task. In steps 1 and 2, students learn what the task is, and why they were doing it. In step 3, the teacher practises particular skills, helps students recall certain information, or builds students' vocabulary. Students have an opportunity to rehearse how they will go about the task. Lessons are designed to enable students to be successful in achieving the lesson's intents. Consider the following examples of lessons that support a chosen task, intent, and set of criteria.

In the art class

Task: To draw a flower

Intent: To look carefully at what we draw

Criteria: Lots of detail in the student drawing

Lesson: The teacher sits with the students and, as a class, they look at a series of calendar pictures of flowers. The teacher asks each student to share in turn what they see in the pictures. The teacher is helping the students practise how to look carefully at a picture.

In a writing time

Task: To write a thank-you note to a museum after a field trip

Intent: To show in the letter how much fun we had

Criteria: Write about (or draw) three things you enjoyed

Lesson: The teacher helps the students create a list on chart paper of all the things they enjoyed. The format for a thank-you letter is briefly reviewed. A template for a thank-you letter is on a separate piece of chart paper.

In math class

Task: To use manipulatives to create number sentences

Intent: To see there are multiple ways of creating number sentences

Criteria: Show at least three ways of forming the number 5 using two numbers

Lesson: With the students gathered around, the teacher shows the class the number family 5 through a collection of objects such as straws or a large image of one die. The teacher asks individual students to come forward and show how they would form the number 5 using two numbers. The teacher then asks, "Who can show us another way?" After each student demonstration, the teacher identifies how the student made each number sentence differently.

In our three examples, the lesson helps students know how to go about their work for the particular task, intent, and criteria. In the first example, the students need to know how to look carefully. In the second example, they need to be helped to remember important details about their trip, and in the last example, the teacher helps stimulate their number sense.

There are two important benefits when teachers use their lessons to show students how to do something. The first result is that the lesson becomes much shorter. In our observations, teachers spend much too long on the lesson because they haven't carefully thought about what they want their students to learn. They try to cover too much ground and the lessons become too detailed and too long. When teachers use intent and criteria to decide what to emphasize and repeat for the students, their teaching becomes more efficient.

The well-defined criteria items and the intent become the main points of the lesson. Because the teacher has narrowed the teaching to specific points, the lesson can be covered in a relatively short time. Less time is spent on explanation and more time is left for the students to work on the task. In assessment for learning classrooms, lessons become "laser-like" (Susan Bukta, grade 2 teacher, in conversation). The reward for teachers and students is that more students complete assignments successfully.

We asked a group of N–3 teachers to think about their experiences with steps 1–3 of the scaffolding for assessment for learning. We asked them three simple questions: "What did you try?" "Did it work?" and "How do you know?" Here are the responses from a few of the primary teachers.

I made up a chart to show steps needed in completing a journal page. Children were often showing me incomplete journal pages. This also caused interruptions during small-group lessons. We went over each step together and did an actual run-through so children understood the chart. Children used the chart on their own. If the odd child showed me an incomplete journal page, I just pointed in the direction of the chart.

Yes, it worked. The journal pages were completed more efficiently. Some comments from children viewing the chart: "Oops, I forgot to colour," "Yes, I'm all done," "I don't even have to use the chart anymore."

I know it worked because of children's comments.

I know it worked because of the journal page completion.

I know it worked because children used it.

It was probably most effective with those who worked at assignments very quickly and students who needed to focus.

– Bev Klowak, grade 1

For an art lesson, I gave the task, intent, and criteria. My expectation was to eliminate statements like: "Is this good or good enough?" "Am I done?" "I'm no good in art." I also wanted students to feel free to explore the use of the materials, not have the piece of produced artwork define and evaluate the student ("Mine sucks!" "I can't draw.").

Yes it worked!!

The students were more engaged in the activity. Very few students came to me with unfinished work. Students began helping each other, showing, commenting, even demonstrating (spontaneously). Everyone was able to fulfill the requirements, which were clear, simple, and precise. The "evaluation" was of the criteria, not the students or their ability. The quality of the art produced was higher. The class was relaxed, focused, cooperative. Students were able to comment on the collection of work in terms of the criteria.

– Susan Bukta, grade 3

These two teachers' comments show that the students and the teachers were pleased with the success that followed from working through steps 1–3. The success of students' daily experiences is an essential part in developing student learners. Students come to know they are successful learners in multiple experiences. They begin to say, "I can do this," "I'm on target," and "I am a successful learner." Setting clear targets helps students experience success each day. Upon reflection, students can see these successes and use them to form a picture of themselves as independent learners.

Support: An Essay

The quality of our achievements in Feedback for Learning was due to the dedication of the teachers involved and the support they received. The teachers we worked with carried the main responsibility for developing and changing their own practice. Much of the work they did was on their own. They did the reading, they did the thinking, they implemented the ideas, and they found the energy to maintain their regular classroom obligations. We were able to support these teachers in several ways.

We recognize that teachers have little influence over the extent or quality of the support available to them, but a good skill is to recognize effective support and adjust your expectations accordingly.

It is possible to achieve a level of success by working alone and using the steps outlined in this book as a resource. You will see gains in student performance and your students will grow as student learners. You will have to persevere on your own to sustain your interest over the length of time it will take to explore these ideas fully.

Support from several different administrative levels can give you materials, time to think, and conversations that will stimulate your progress. From the point of view of the teachers in the Feedback for Learning project, the most obvious support came from conversations with two distinct support people. One was from outside the district and the other was already a teacher in the district. Having these two types of support people proved to be very effective.

The specialist from outside the district, Ruth Sutton, had a deep understanding of assessment and an extensive knowledge of the supporting research. Ruth was able to share this expertise directly with teachers in a manner that made teachers feel she was a colleague and a friend. Ruth made it clear at the planning stage that implementing new assessment practices was also about changing teacher behaviours and that we must treat teachers as adult learners. These ideas were carefully considered and became major components of the program.

The second support person, Thompson Owens, had worked with many of the teachers for some time and had built up a rapport and trust with them. In conversations with teachers, Thompson brought his understanding of how students learn and how educational systems work.

In the beginning, Thompson played the role of project manager: arranging schedules and helping Ruth understand the nuances of the district. Since Ruth only visited the district three times a year, Thompson maintained continuity with teachers and administrators in the interim, troubleshooting and having ongoing conversations with teachers. As time progressed, Thompson played more of the consultant role to teachers and administrators.

At least one of the support people tried to meet with the teachers about every six to eight weeks. In these conversations the support people concentrated on listening to the teachers. They used their understanding and experience to ask questions that would help teachers focus on critical issues.

The consultants avoided handing out activities or giving advice. The support teachers assumed that most teachers probably have more activities stuffed away in cupboards than they could ever use anyway. It is not the activity that is so important, it is the ability to think like the person who created the activity.

Advice had limited value, especially when neither support person had any primary teaching experience. Each classroom is a unique blend of the school milieu, the particular students, and the particular teacher. Advice is an easy answer that may have worked in another context but will almost never fit a particular teacher's personality, talents, or needs.

The next important level of support for the teachers we worked with came from the school administrators, such as the principals and vice-principals. The administrators remained visible but stayed on the sidelines most of the time. They did not try to micro-manage the teachers. They showed their support through informal discussions and questions. Administrators promoted teacher discussions. They scheduled the meetings and found the funding to cover missed classes. Teachers were able to have conversations with the consultants and not be distracted by their busy classrooms. Later, discussions were arranged between staff members.

The administrators who worked with teachers in the Feedback for Learning project were patient and enthusiastic. They were anxious for results but respected the learning process for their teachers by giving them years to make progress in the new assessment practices. Finally, administrators showed support to their teachers by applying the principles of Feedback for Learning to their own practice. They treated themselves as learners and asked, "How can I apply the principles of good assessment to my work as a school leader?" This sent a powerful message to their teachers that the work on assessment was important.

Most teachers do not think of their superintendents as being a support because they seldom have the opportunity to work directly with them. In the Winnipeg school district where Feedback for Learning occurred, the superintendent, Pauline Clarke, was an important support, and she played several key roles in our project. At the start-up stage, Pauline made sure that there were clear targets, and that funding and support people were in place. As the program developed, Pauline found time to meet with the key people to listen and ask questions. The questions helped the project organizers think carefully and develop a more balanced program. Pauline was careful to follow the learning process, allowing schools to choose to participate. She was also crucial in ensuring that the program continued over a number of years and developed a sustainability plan to allow the changes to become permanent.

You may not have all these people to help support radical changes to assessment practice in your school or school system, but you will probably be able to find some support. For example:

- Are your friends willing to work with you on assessment?

- Are there colleagues, other than personal friends, who might be interested in working with you on this topic? They do not necessarily have to be in your school.

- Are there consultants in your district who might be willing to coach you? They do not necessarily have to be experts in assessment, but they do have to know how to listen and how to use questions to help clarify your thinking.

- Is your administrator open to requests for time to meet with colleagues? Can they help you find the funding?

- How might your superintendent react to a letter outlining what you plan to do, your intent, and your self-evaluation scheme?

Review your support options and rate your situation. If some support is not in place, how can you adapt? Support, purpose, and determination will help you as you embark on changing your assessment practice. The ideas suggested above helped with the Feedback for Learning project, and ideally, in order for the changes to be sustainable, support is important. Others will want participate when they realize the drastic changes in student success as they become independent student learners, thanks to assessment for learning.

4

SMALL Rs

In short, the dialogue between pupils and a teacher should be thoughtful, reflective, focused to evoke and explore understanding, and conducted so that all pupils have an opportunity to think and to express their ideas.

– Black and Wiliam, 1998

Guiding Questions

1. How would you treat the student who frequently has very little work completed as a student learner?

2. In assessment for learning classrooms, when is it correct to just tell a student what to do?

3. How will you get feedback for yourself on how long you wait for student responses?

Key Ideas of Chapter Four

- steps 4–7 transfer the responsibility for solving problems to the student

- steps 4–7 are a structure for the daily conversations between teacher and students

- an invitation must be respectful of the learner

- thinking takes time. Students need to be given time to respond

- teachers must restate the thinking process for the student

Introduction

Students need many opportunities each day to experience reflective behaviour such as hearing others making reflective statements, reading statements shared by other students, being guided by teachers, and watching or listening to the teacher as they coach other students. Each one of these experiences is a mini-reflection, a "small r," that adds to the students' metacognitive concepts and language. The accumulation of these experiences prepares students to be successful in the final step of the scaffolding (see figure 1.3), reflection.

Steps 4–7 of the scaffolding for assessment for learning are all designed to help teachers provide students with daily reflective experiences with solving problems. Following this sequence of steps helps students to critically compare their work to a target model, and then adjust it to meet the target.

As we described in chapter 3, it is essential that students have clear tasks, intents, and criteria (TICs) in order to become independent learners. Setting clear targets helps more students experience success. The daily successes provide multiple examples for students when they are asked to reflect on what they can do well.

Steps 4–7 provide a guide for teachers who want to coach their students to be independent as they improve their own work and solve their problems. It may seem easy for a teacher to tell students what to do. With the target clearly in mind, a teacher might simply direct students on how to improve their work: "A capital is missing here." "You have missed something there." "Look at that line again." These statements direct students towards the target task and their work will end up being of high quality. If the teacher does this, however, the students are not required to rethink their work in terms of the target. The teacher has done the thinking for them, has spotted the errors, and moved the student along to a conclusion. While this is very efficient and many very good products will be created, the student is not being taught to be self-reflective.

Students from nursery school to grade 3 are just beginning to form the basic attitudes towards how they will deal with problems that continue throughout their school careers. Grades N–3 students need to be directed towards the thinking processes that build and reinforce their confidence in their own ability to deal with any learning challenge.

Steps 4–7

In the assessment for learning scaffolding, steps 4–7 transform the students into independent learners by helping transfer ownership of the learning from the teacher to the student. The teacher first establishes what the student has done well and recognizes their achievements. The student is invited to compare her/his work to the criteria or model. Students are responsible for choosing the next steps, however small the steps may be. The teacher commends the student for acting like a learner and choosing how to improve the outcome. The students feel successful because of the increased self-esteem that comes from ownership of their actions.

We see steps 4–7 of the scaffolding as the bridge connecting a teacher's guidance in setting the learning targets (steps 1–3) to the students' awareness of themselves as learners (step 8).

Step 4 Provide a first attempt for the students to show what they know.

Step 5 Invite comparison.

Step 6 Have students identify the next step(s).

Step 7 Provide an opportunity for a second attempt to reach the goals, using the chosen next step.

These four steps are the most difficult steps on the scaffolding. Teachers become frustrated when students simply do not seem interested in improving their work, even when the teachers are diligent about making the targets clear and inviting their students to help create the list of criteria for success. Teachers are often tempted to make things easier, and will suggest that students simply move on. Steps 5–7 are designed to help delicately pass on the responsibility for learning from the teacher to the student.

Consider the following classroom example of a conversation between a teacher and a student. The teacher has given her grade 3 students a variety of calendar photos of flowers and asked them to draw one of them. The students spent some time as a group looking closely at the photographs before they started working on their drawings. After working for some time, they were invited to line up to talk to the teacher about each drawing. Here is one of the conversations between a student and his teacher about his flower drawing.

Teacher: Let's look together at your drawing. Which part looks most like the calendar picture?

Student:	This part (pointing to the petals).
Teacher:	Yes, I see that.
Teacher:	You know, I like the edges you have drawn. They are kind of bumpy like the edges of the flower. Which part was hardest for you to draw?
Student:	All the petals.
Teacher:	Do you see this part of the flower (pointing to the centre of the flower)? In a real flower you could poke your finger down right inside. How could you draw going inside?
Student:	(Long silence as the student thinks of a response)
Teacher:	What do you see in the photograph?
Student:	(Looking more closely)
Teacher:	What do you see going inside?
Student:	Lines.
Teacher:	Yes, there are some lines. I wonder if you could try to draw these lines in your flower.
Student:	(Nods)

– Susan Butka and a grade 3 student

A similar conversational pattern was repeated with all the students as they showed the teacher their drawings. Now, let's see how the conversation fits the frame in steps 4–7.

Step 4   The students have had an opportunity to work on their drawings after a lesson on how to look closely at the photographs.

Step 5   The teacher offers an invitation: "Let's look at the picture together." The comparison is toward the target, which is the photograph of the flower the student is drawing.

Step 6   After helping the student identify a possible next step (e.g., adding more lines), the teacher offers a choice: "I wonder if you could try drawing these lines in your picture." The student agrees.

Step 7   The student goes back to his desk and works on adding more lines to his drawing.

By listening carefully to the student and asking questions, the teacher can focus the student's thinking so that the solutions come from the student, not the teacher. The student has experienced a small *r, reflection.* Reflection is the form of one opportunity for the student to review the work and choose the next step with coaching from the teacher. As teachers repeat these kinds of conversations, students build a repertoire of how to reflect on their work and how to choose appropriate next steps. In the teacher/student conversation above, the teacher has transferred the responsibility of finding solutions to the student. We have called the teacher/student conversations *learning conversations.*

Learning conversations

These short conversations between teachers and students happen often throughout the school day and are opportunities for students to have mini-reflections about their learning. The transfer of responsibility to students for their learning is not just a behaviour change for students; it is a change in the way they think. A conversation between teacher and students that is designed to help the student think is a learning conversation. The Learning Conversation Frame (see figure 4.1) outlines the basic elements of an exchange that will help students think about their work. Teachers can use the framework as a guide to talking to students.

Learning Conversation Frame

Beginning the Conversation: Inviting

1. Body position open
2. Voice open
   • Tone
   • Word choice
3. Problem restated

Questioning: Allowing Time for Thinking/Comparing

4. Clarifying the problem/issue
5. Turning attention to
   • TIC
   • Wall chart
   • Other classroom resources

6. Wait time

Concluding the Conversation: The Language of Reflection

7. Rephrasing by
   • Teacher
   • Student

Figure 4.1 Learning Conversation Frame.

Beginning the Conversation: The Invitation to Think

In starting conversations with students, we suggest that the initial step is for teachers to establish respect for the students. We all know that primary-aged students will immediately sense when a teacher is not genuine, and if there is no trust between the student and teacher, then there will be no productive learning conversation. In the invitation to think, teachers can rephrase the student's statements to show that the teacher understands the student's concerns or problems. When the teacher repeats things back to the student, it reinforces that she understands what the student is saying, but it also promotes respect.

> Teachers may want to read Costa and Garmston (2002). The Cognitive Coaching program helped clarify thinking about conversations that lead students to be independent learners.

Questions for Comparison: Allowing Students Time to Think

Students are asked to think about possible resources available to them that are in the classroom. When questioning students, one of the biggest challenges for teachers is to wait for the student to respond after they have asked their question. Waiting for a reply takes a great deal of practice on the part of the teacher.

For many very good reasons, wait time after questions is abandoned by teachers. Invariably, when we've asked teachers about waiting for the students to answer, they shake their heads and smile in recognition of the need for waiting and the recognition that they don't wait long enough. We believe one of the reasons teachers do not wait for students to respond is that they want their students to succeed and that if a student does not answer the question in less than a second or two, the teacher asks another question, and then another, in an effort to help the student find the right words. Unfortunately, this only results in confusing the young student, whose brain does not work as quickly as an adult's and is, as a result, still thinking about the first question when the third and fourth are being asked. They just get more confused about what they are being asked. With this frustration, the teacher usually ends up telling the student what to do, but it is often phrased like a suggestion: "Do you think you could ...?" The student understands this as a command, coded in teacher talk, not an invitation to the student to decide on their own course of action. The teacher first needs to help the student clarify what the problem is. Some good questions to ask might include:

- Can you tell me what's wrong?
- What's the problem?
- Where are you stuck?

Once the teacher asks a question, the key is to STOP talking. Do not immediately add to the questions or try to clarify anything. This will just result in further confusing the student. We suggest that teachers recite this tag in their heads at the end of asking any question to students: "And now I'm going to stop talking for five seconds, to give you a chance to respond." This will remind the teacher that a question is meant to be an invitation for the student to think and that a response will take a little time to formulate. The length of time a teacher has to wait for a response may be much longer than five seconds. Even if the teacher waits, the student's explanation of the problem may be very general. The teacher can help the student at this point by rephrasing his/her statements and gently probing with further questions until both the teacher and student feel they have zeroed in on the problem.

After the student has answered the question, the teacher's next step is to turn the student's attention to classroom resources that might help them solve their problem. One of the first resources to explore is the original instruction given to the student. The nature of the questioning should be framed positively so that it builds on the student's strengths. Ask questions such as, "When we started, we talked about what to do. Can you tell me what you remember?" In a similar way, teachers can invite students to think about other resources in the classroom that they might find useful, such as strategy lists, vocabulary lists, or student samples. They can base their next step on the most appropriate resource for each student. If teachers think of the questions in terms of drawing the students' attention to the resources, or as reminders of what is available, the questions will be framed positively and will be heard by students as invitations, not commands or directives. Often, students need help learning how to look at a resource. The teacher may have to direct a student's attention to particular aspects of the instructions to help the student concentrate.

Concluding the Conversation: Building the Language of Reflection

Concluding the conversation should help lead the student to developing the language of reflection. Once the problem is clearly visible to the student, the problem disappears, and his/her attention immediately switches to setting to work to fix the problem. The student's mind jumps from stuck to unstuck without any intervening time spent thinking about what just happened. It is important at this point to help the student reflect on how the problem was solved before he/she moves on to the task itself. The teacher can take a moment to ask, "So how did you solve (or, are you going to solve) the problem?" One teacher we worked with asked her students to restate their answers in an effort to help them associate the language of problem solving with the activity of reflection and help them learn the language of reflection. She asked her students, "Just so I know that you and I agree, can you tell me what the solution is?"

The Learning Conversation Frame (see figure 4.1) helps teachers see what is involved in productive conversations with students. The framework provides an entry point for teachers to put in place the important ideas of student/teacher rapport and wait-time questioning. We suggest making one copy of the framework to help keep track of the conversations with students, and to keep the talk on track. Often the teacher realizes that the problems facing students come from something that is unclear or missing in the original instructions. Keeping this in mind, it is helpful to think about this framework as teachers begin their lesson plans, and think from this perspective in every stage of the lesson. Listening to the students will help teachers make the intent or criteria of the task more specific.

Step 4: Provide a first attempt for the students to show what they know

The first attempt at completing a task generally occurs after the teacher stops giving their instructions or lessons. The lesson has been taught, the task, intent, and criteria have been written out, and the questions have been discussed. Pencils are sharpened and students are ready to start working. Students must have an opportunity to begin the task and complete as much as they can on their own.

Students may be slow to get started, and may be easily distracted from the task. The result is that even though the teacher has allowed a reasonable amount of time for students to begin their task, they may achieve very little, or nothing. Still, this initial effort counts as a first attempt, even if the student has not really started the assignment or has only completed a minimal amount. The teachable moment here shifts from the task itself to a more general problem of how to get started.

A first attempt does not imply that the students should complete the task before the teacher intervenes. Primary teachers know that young students need to be asked questions about their work while they are in the middle of the process. Asking primary students why they did something a few days after the event is usually not helpful. However, if you ask a student to talk about what they are thinking while they are in the process of working, they are more likely to be able to talk about their thought process.

The biggest problem in implementing this step is usually stopping teachers from interacting with their students – even for a few moments – after the lesson was complete. As the students moved from having the assignment explained to working on the task, the teacher is often up, standing close to the students, and, in an encouraging, reassuring manner, reviewing the task yet again. This is distracting and confusing to students.

Though this shows that teachers are driven by their care, compassion, and sense of professional responsibility to their students, and makes for successful completion of assignments, it does little to help students be independent learners. Students need time to get stuck and to realize that they have a problem that needs to be sorted out. Step 4 is meant to give students permission, in as safe an environment as possible, to come up against problems as they work.

We suggest two ways to get teachers to stand back and let their students work until they encounter problems.

- The **Two-Minute Sweep**   Teachers should tell the students, "No questions for two minutes, please." During the two minutes, teachers should sweep their eyes around the class – without commenting on the assignment – and just observe the students.

  Teachers should be looking for success, for example, students who are on-task and students who are doing exactly what the assignment requires. These should be careful observations and teachers should note exactly what the students are doing that is successful. When the two minutes are up, the teacher should go over to at least three students and compliment them. Their comments should be specific instead of general comments. Statements such as, "Good job" or "Way to go" are not constructive for young students, and they do not have any direction for students. More specific comments such as, "You have a date on your paper just like we decided," or "I noticed you shared a pencil with your classmate. We said we should be helping each other and you did that by sharing," are much more useful for students as they work to become independent learners.

- **Survey** is another tool that we like to use to help distract teachers from solving their students' problems too quickly. In this exercise, teachers record their observations about student learning. They can guide their observations using a set of questions. The questions will differ, depending on the needs of the class. We suggest beginning the observation and recording process with the following questions:

  – What evidence is there about the preferred learning modalities of your students?

  – What evidence is there of student understanding?

  – What are student attitudes toward the task?

These systematic observations can form the basis of teachers' decisions about adapting their approach to meet their students' needs.

Step 5: Invite comparison

There are only two words in this step but each carries several implications. The word *invite* was carefully chosen to reflect more respect for the learner. Students need to feel that the teacher is supportive, and not judgmental. For teachers, it is easy to go wrong here. It is common for teachers to want to make statements but phrase them as questions. Consider the following scenario:

> The students have been assigned a writing task and are casually getting down to work and seem not to be committed to the task. There is never as much time as the teacher would like so the teacher cruises through the classroom, patiently, but firmly, trying to settle the students down to work. As the teacher passes one student, she notices that the student is well into the writing but there is no title to the work. During the lesson, the importance of a title had been thoroughly discussed and all the students had nodded in agreement and understanding. The teacher uses a question to draw the student's attention to the omission: "What about a title?"

In such a scenario, students understand such questions as directives to change something, not invitations to look at their work critically. A true invitation is worded in such a way as to allow for several responses and assumes the student has the resources to answer the question. A teacher may also invite students to reflect by presenting a variety of ways for the students to improve their work. At a good buffet, the arrangement of the food invites you to choose what you want and appeals to a variety of tastes and appetites. In the same way, teachers can invite students to improve their work by presenting a variety of options that will appeal to various levels and abilities. In the above scenario, the teacher might instead have said, "I see you have already done quite a bit. What will you have to do to finish?" This question provides more options for the student. The student can think back to the lesson and then discuss what was important in the writing assignment. The student may recall the importance of including a title and, if not, the teacher can remind him/her.

The second word of step 5, *comparison*, also needs attention. When we *compare,* we judge something against something else. While mature learners have developed mental models of correct spellings and reasonable estimations of math problems, younger learners have not. The process of comparison is not automatic for young students, as they have no such models in their heads against which to compare. They need concrete models or examples against which to compare their work. The process of comparison can be against a given model, or it can be to the criteria that were established at the beginning of the lesson.

Comparison is a higher level thinking skill in Bloom's ranking of thinking processes. A young student will need training and practice to learn how to look carefully at models and compare them to their own work to see similarities and differences.

Step 6: Have students identify the next step(s)

This step makes clear that assessment for learning requires the student (not the teacher) to choose what must be changed or modified. To be successful with step 6, the student thinks through possible choices. This requires enough time, which is often more time than most teachers feel they can afford to spend with one student.

Any student will take much longer than a teacher would to decide what needs to be improved in his/her work. With deadlines looming and with students all finishing at different times, teachers will feel intense pressure to just tell students what needs to be improved rather than spend time letting them decide on their own. When the teacher tells the student what to improve, the result is a quicker and perhaps better product, but it does not help the student become an independent learner.

The word *identify* implies that the student has a variety of options. The identification of the next step comes after the student sees clearly that there are a variety of ways to proceed or improve his/her work. The next step for some students may be to spend more time trying to solve a problem, but with a new approach. It may be appropriate to choose a favourite strategy to help their thinking. They may want to talk to a friend, use a word web, or refer to a wall chart in the classroom. Although the teachers are not as involved in this step, their behaviours are important to helping the student make choices about the next steps. The teacher needs to be patient, positive, and able to use questions to help the students focus.

Step 7: Provide an opportunity for a second attempt to reach the goal(s), using the chosen next step

Steps 6 and 7 should always happen one after the other. The teacher works with all the students in the class, or with a single student, to help with the process of identifying areas to improve. Students can then immediately make the improvements to their work. The student learns that their actions can help improve their work and that success is not a chance occurrence that is beyond their control. It is a result of her/his actions.

> For many ideas to help record student reflective thinking, we highly recommend the series of books on assessment by Gregory, Cameron, and Davies (1997, 2000, 2001). Teachers we worked with found them very useful.

Wall expectations

One of the best ways to help teachers transfer responsibility for learning to students is with *wall expectations*. Teachers put up a chart on the wall of what they want their students to learn. A TIC chart (see chapter 2) is a good example of this. The task, intent, and criteria are the teacher's best attempt to make the daily learning task clear to the student. In chart form, it is easy for students to refer to on their own to remind themselves of what is expected. Teachers can also use the TIC chart to give students a way to help themselves decide what to do next.

When a student is stuck, the temptation for the teacher is to solve the problem for them and get the student back on track. Classrooms are very busy places and operate at several levels all at once. The teacher has to pay attention to everything, even when one of the students asks a question about their work. It is difficult for a teacher to focus on one child when two in the corner are arguing over the use of scissors, another is sad because a playmate won't listen, and another is acting out a movie scene that even the teacher found too violent. Despite this reality, teachers can train themselves to help students reflect by structuring the conversations. Consider the following conversation between a student and her teacher.

Student: I don't know what to do.

Teacher: Let's see what you have so far. (Looking at the child's paper and nodding) Do you remember the instructions?

Student: (Turning his head to the wall chart where the TICs are recorded)

Teacher: Tell me what you remember.

Student: (Thinking first for six to eight seconds, then, with eyes raised, lists several points)

Teacher: That's very good. (With an eye on the rest of the class) Let's go look at the instructions. (They walk over to the TICs wall chart) You remembered these two criteria. (Pointing with her finger) Do you remember what this criterion was?

Student: Student reads from the chart. (Again, pauses to make sense of it. Then, obviously understanding what to do, starts to walk back to finish the work)

Teacher: (Calling the student back) Just to review; tell me how you solved the problem.

Student: I looked at the paper.

Teacher: (Rephrasing) I agree. You had done most of the work already but when you were stuck you looked at the list and then you knew what to do. You've done a very good job solving your problem.

The teacher did not exactly answer the student's question but she helped the student remember a resource that could help her solve the problem. The student experienced basic reflective skills: looking at her work and deciding whether it met the criteria. Repetition of these skills will be necessary before they become a solid strategy in the student's repertoire.

Let's look again at steps 4–7 and review the above conversation within the framework of the scaffolding.

Step 4: Students make a first attempt at the work. The students are busy working on the assigned task and there are several levels of success. The teacher is moving throughout the class and is available to students as they work. One student approaches with a question.

Step 5: The teacher invites comparison to the description of the task on the wall chart. To make it an invitation and not a command, the teacher begins positively by asking, "What do you remember?" She praises the student for what she already understands and has under control. Then the teacher takes her student over to the list and directs the student's attention to what is written down. Only then does the teacher point to the missing criterion in the student's work.

Step 6 and **Step 7:** The student makes a choice and acts upon the decision. In our scenario, the student wants to get back to work as soon as she sees what is missing. This will often happen. Students will automatically want to work on tasks they believe they can accomplish. If the student still does not understand the listed criterion, the teacher can spend more time making it clear.

The scripted conversation above might last between one and two minutes. This may seem like a great deal of time to spend with one student but the lesson extends much further. Teachers who have tried this method of conversation find that many of the other students listen to the conversation and learn how to handle their own problems without asking the teacher. Many students in the class learn that they do not have to ask the teacher when they can refer to the criteria listed on a wall chart. These students will inform their classmates about how to use the criteria list. The ripple effect from the conversation between one student and the teacher ends up saving the teacher from having to repeat the scenario over and over again with each student.

The process of transferring responsibility begins when the teacher puts up the criteria for the task in a visible place for all students to see. This forces the students to see that there are options, aside from asking the teacher, and helps move students toward being independent learners who can solve their own problems.

Creating a list of problem-solving strategies is another very useful way to use wall expectations (see figure 4.2). The intent here is to expand the students' repertoires of ways to help themselves, beyond simply asking the teacher or using the TIC sheets. As these strategies are introduced, practised, and discussed throughout the term, a strategy list is compiled on large chart paper and displayed in the classroom. We usually include "word webs" and "ask a friend" on the strategy list. As students work in different subject areas, different problem-solving strategies will arise and these too can be added to the list. Having a great variety of strategies is best for students.

The wall chart of strategies becomes a resource in itself that students use to help themselves when they do not know what to do next. Unless teachers direct students to use the wall charts, though, the wall chart will become just wallpaper.

- look at charts
- read the instructions
- think about what you learned before and how you can use it
- look around the class for clues
- look in a dictionary
- stop and think
- draw a picture
- think about the problem and try a different strategy
- sound it out
- look for smaller words within bigger words
- use a brochure for information

Figure 4.2 Wall expectations list of strategies. *Lyn Peterson and Patricia Deluca, grade 2.*

If a student asks the teacher a question after working on an assignment independently for a while, the teacher must decide if the student has understood the task in the first place. If the student is clear about the instructions, but is still stuck, the teacher can invite comparison to the wall charts of thinking strategies. The invitation to think about the chart begins with asking the student what they have tried already, implying that the student has previously tried every other possible approach before coming to the teacher.

The tone of the question and the teacher's body language are as important as the words he/she uses. The basic message, in the phrasing and tone of the question and the teacher's body language, should be that it is okay to have a problem. The message we want to give to students is that we are all learners, we all get stuck, and, if we are learning something new, we will run into problems.

The comparison the teacher makes in step 5 is to the list of strategies compiled on the wall chart. Ask students, "Do you think you can find a strategy that might help your thinking?" "Have you got another strategy that you might try next?" Some students will need the teacher to go over the lists and strategies with them. Others may only need a reminder to check that resource themselves. The student chooses from the list of familiar strategies in step 6 and then uses that strategy in step 7. The strategy list becomes a problem-solving resource for students to refer to as an alternative to asking the teacher.

Each time the teacher patiently leads the student through this process, the students are practising reflective thinking. Students learn that when they are confronted with a problem, they can use a variety of strategies to solve it. Repetition will help them develop this pattern of thinking as a habit and it will become second nature for them.

Choice is the key to the successful use of wall charts. Students must make their own choices, but the teacher can narrow these choices so the process is within the student's ability. When the overall intent is to create student learners, the particular choices students make are less important than the fact that they actually made the decision on their own.

The criteria for designing good targets are clarity and manageability. First of all, it must be clear to the students what their choices are. Secondly, the choices must be rich enough but not too broad so the choice is real to the student.

We have often heard teachers say to the class, "Begin your work and if you have problems, ask two friends first and then ask me." Does this directive help students become independent learners? Students are being asked to use their classmates as a resource and they will often find the help they need before they go to the teacher. So, this is a successful strategy for students to use. They are given permission to share ideas with their friends and are learning how to use the valuable strategy as an alternative to asking the teacher. In terms of the scaffolding, however, giving the students the directive to ask two friends and then the teacher falls short because the students are not given any opportunity to choose their own best strategy to help themselves become independent learners.

At the early stages of introducing a new strategy, it is reasonable for students to use the one strategy until they fully understand it. Students can spend time as a class analyzing what makes the strategy work well, and what its shortcomings are. Once they agree, they can add the strategy to the growing list of ways to help themselves solve problems.

We suggest teachers incorporate the process of making wall expectations lists in the lesson-planning phase. Making it an outcome of the unit will help teachers stay focused on keeping up the lists throughout the year. Plan for wall charts of vocabulary lists, key ideas, and important questions, and include a strategies list as one of the charts.

Collegiality: An Essay

Teaching is a lonely job. When you close the door to your classroom, the success of the students lies directly on your shoulders. Most of the time, having the responsibility for the group of learners is a rewarding challenge. In the classroom, there are multiple opportunities to experience the world of the child through conversations with your students. But, there is also a need for adult conversation.

Adult learners need to be able to talk with colleagues in order to develop in their profession. Thoughts that are a jumble of emotions, reactions, and intent become clearer as you try to express them in the linear fashion of a conversation. Conversations that enhance your learning should be thoughtful and reflective about your job. You must feel you are being listened to, respected, and supported.

There are times in your teaching career when you are blessed with the wonderful happenstance of working alongside a soulmate, a person who shares many of your values and dreams for teaching. Such a friend adds a quality to your workplace that cannot be measured. You can express your frustration, confusion, and excitement, and know that your feelings will be met with sympathy, encouragement, and good humour. These conversations can be very brief and happen during the school day or can be extended planning sessions over weekend getaways.

Not all your professional relationships will be this special, nor do they need to be. It is still possible to have rich and meaningful dialogue with colleagues who have different responsibilities or experiences but are sympathetic and want to learn about their profession.

You will not grow as a teacher if you do not have many opportunities to talk over your ideas with a variety of colleagues. Reading educational materials and working by yourself can only take you so far. It is difficult to step outside yourself, pause, and ask, "What have I learned?" A group of colleagues can help you analyze the problems you face, sharpen your understanding, and, just as importantly, they can help you celebrate your successes.

Formal opportunities that allow teachers to engage in reflective conversations are rare. There are many times when a teacher can grab moments from their daily obligations to exchange a few words with a co-worker, but there are very few times when teachers are permitted to sit with colleagues and reflect on the effectiveness of their programs or the nuances of their mandate.

Momentary exchanges while you are between tasks or the students are out at recess do not count as opportunities to learn. You cannot have really meaningful dialogue while you are in the classroom, even if the students are engaged in some project work. There are too many distractions for the conscientious teacher. Staff meetings are not an ideal time, either. These meetings usually occur at the end of the day, when you have already expended much of your energy teaching, and often have packed agendas that must be covered in short periods of time.

The talk must occur when you are rested and without distractions, and be long enough that you can delve into the topic. We suggest putting aside at least 30 minutes. With these conditions, you have a chance to begin thinking about your practice.

From time to time, teachers are given opportunities to share ideas at in-service days and, infrequently, meetings are scheduled during the regular school days. The learning can be removed from these opportunities for discussion if the meetings have been over-organized or are about administrative issues. Often these meetings are chaired by an administrator and are structured around the need to organize specific school events. Interesting conversations such as on-topic personal asides or exploration of interesting sidebars are kept to a minimum. Meetings organized in this way have administrative value but do not really help teachers learn their craft.

Collegial conversations for teacher learning require a different structure. The general responsibility for the discussion should lie with the group. The chairperson has the permission of the participants to bring everyone back on topic but is not too authoritative. The tone of the meeting allows the participants to talk about the issues that they face, their stumbling blocks, and their frustrations.

In these very democratic conversations, ideas flow back and forth in a spirit of camaraderie. They are driven by a sense of inquiry into an area in which all the participants are interested. Teachers want to know what is going on in other classrooms. They want to know, "How is it organized?" "What topics are being covered at the moment?" "What are you trying that is successful?" As these ideas emerge, each teacher's understanding of the topic deepens. These conversations can be very exciting and rewarding for each individual. Conversations like these leave teachers with a sense that they know more about their craft.

Another teacher-support conversation is one where one teacher takes on the role of a mentor, coach, or a lead teacher. Most teachers shy away from this role because it sounds as if they are calling themselves a *master teacher* who will dispense wisdom to other teachers.

A coaching conversation between two colleagues deepens understanding by helping the teacher look back on their work and reflect. Teachers can take turns being the coach/listener and the teacher/speaker. These conversations should also take place outside the classroom, free of distractions, rather than in a busy staffroom at lunch hour.

The listener is not there to give advice but to help make the options clearer. Not having to give advice relieves the listener from the responsibility of providing the right answer. The listener is allowed to paraphrase what is said and to use questions to help the teacher be more specific and help the teacher see what options are available.

The teacher who is speaking chooses the topic and agrees to avoid asking for solutions. Most teachers struggle to avoid asking for advice. Teachers who are really tired or under the pressure of a deadline will resort to, "Just tell me what to do!"

This model is also a safe way for teachers to visit each other's classroom. In this case the coach/listener watches and possibly gathers data on some issue identified by the teacher/speaker. After the observation, the only responsibility of the coach/listener is to report what was seen or to hand over the data collected. There is no need for the coach/listener to give judgments because their only responsibility is to provide another set of eyes. The purpose of the coach/listener model is to clarify the teacher's thinking. Ultimately, this is the best model since it leads the teachers to discover answers for themselves.

All these conversations have their strengths and weaknesses. All are needed if teachers are to develop in their profession as learners.

(These ideas are based on Costa and Garmston, 2002.)

APPENDICES

REPRODUCIBLES

Appendix I:
Measuring Impact Form

Teacher:_____

School:_____   Grade:_____

1. What did you do? _____
   _____
   _____
   _____

2. To what extent did it work? _____
   _____
   _____
   _____

3. How do you know? (You may wish to include a description of the types
   of students who were most affected.)_____
   _____
   _____
   _____

4. Attachments: (work samples, marks, tape recording, videotapes, student-
   written comments, TA comments) _____
   _____
   _____
   _____

Appendix 2:
Short Planning Sheet for Scaffolding Assessment

Questions	Comments
Step 1: • The learning task and learning intent (why)	
Step 2: • How will task/intent be shared? • How will student ideas be recorded? • My own key criteria:	
Step 3: • Some enabling tasks to help students learn:	
Step 4: • How much time is allowed for students' first attempt?	
Step 5: • How will students be encouraged to compare their work to the standard? (worksheet, classmates, teacher) • What will I pay attention to when inviting comparison? (wait time, question type)	
Step 6: • What choices are there for students when they choose their next steps?	
Step 7: • How quickly can next steps be taken?	
Step 8: • How and when will students reflect as learners? • What questions will be asked?	

Appendix 3:
Planning Questions for Teachers

Part One: Getting Yourself Ready

1. What is the task? (Step 1: Task) _____

   _____

2. Why are you asking students to do this task? (Step 1: Intent)

   _____

   _____

3. How will you introduce the task and the intent? (a skit, grade-level presentation, school assembly, guest speaker) (Step 2: Sharing)

   _____

   _____

4. What criteria will indicate success? (Step 2: Sharing)

Looks Like / Sounds Like

What will it look like?	What will it sound like?

5. How will you involve the students in identifying the criteria? _____

6. What images or symbols can be associated with the items on the criteria list?

   _____

   _____

   _____

   _____

7. Where will the criteria sheet be posted in the room? _____

8. What skills will the students need in order to be successful? (Step 3: Enabling)

   _____

   _____

   _____

9. What enabling activities can the students use to learn and practise these skills? (Step 3: Enabling)

Skills	Enabling Activity

Part Two: Helping Students Learn

10. How will you invite students to compare their work with the list called Looks Like/Sounds Like? (Step 5: Invite, and Step 6: Student identifies)

a) Some time after students have started:

• What will you choose to say that is specific, descriptive, and related to the list called Looks Like/Sounds Like?_____

_____

_____

• How will you refer to the list when you ask the student to tell you her/his assessment of his/her work?_____

_____

_____

• How often will you ask students to write their comments down? (consider the learning style of the students, general writing ability)

_____

_____

• How will you help students build the vocabulary they need to record their evaluations? (word lists, model sentences, checklists with icons)

_____

_____

_____

b) After all students have had a chance to continue their work:

• Have a whole-class review of the list called Looks Like/Sounds Like.

• Which items on the list were the easiest to accomplish?_____

_____

- Which items on the list were the most difficult to accomplish?

  _____

  _____

- How might we help ourselves to do better? _____

  _____

  _____

- Are there items to add to or delete from our list? (teachers may also wish to add/delete items) _____

  _____

c) After students have completed their work:

- Ask students to present to one another and take turns pretending to be the teacher, listening to the student reading his/her work. Move through the classroom and note examples of students exhibiting behaviours that are on the target list. Afterwards, the students and teacher report examples of students hitting their target.

- Ask students to present to the class. Ask questions of the students, based on the list Looks Like/Sounds Like.

11. How quickly can you give students an opportunity to practise changing their work? (Step 7: Second attempt)_____

Some suggestions:

- Review with the students as you start the next assignment. Look at the successes, difficulties, and strategies from the previous assignments.

- Present a general issue to the class that you have observed. Ask the class to work in pairs to suggest solutions and share their ideas with the whole class.

- Ask permission to present one student's "difficulty" to the class and have the whole class suggest possible solutions. Then present the class with a similar, but different, "difficulty" and let the students practise one of the solutions in groups.

Part Three: Reviewing the Learning

12. How will you celebrate student progress and deepen their learning?

(Step 8: Student learning) _____

_____

This should occur after the students have worked at several assignments, re-examined their performance, and tried to practise the skills they need to improve. For this to work most efficiently, students should review the accumulated evaluation sheets referred to in Part Two: Helping Students Learn.

• What do you think you do especially well? _____

_____

• Describe the challenges. _____

_____

• What strategies did you choose to help you with the difficult parts? _____

_____

• How well did the strategies work? _____

• What other strategies might you use? _____

_____

• Next time ... _____

_____

_____

Appendix 4:
Rubric for Success: How Am I Doing?

Step 1: Setting Goal(s)	Task and intent not clear	Teacher understands task and intent but these are framed in general terms	Intent and task stated in terms specific enough to guide teaching and assessing*
Step 2: Sharing with Students	Goals not stated	Teacher shares goals with students	Goals have been explained, illustrated, and exemplified in ways appropriate for students' learning profiles**
Step 3: Enabling Tasks	Learning activities do not connect with the learning intent	Some activities directed towards student success in meeting the intended skills and concepts	Most activities enable and encourage students to achieve and demonstrate intended skills and concepts
Step 3: Assessment Criteria	Assessment criteria not shared with students	Teacher provides the assessment criteria	Students are invited to develop criteria through discussion and use of exemplars
Step 4: First Attempt	Students unclear of purpose and criteria	Students clear about purpose, but criteria have not been reviewed	Students clear on purpose of task. Intent and criteria have been reviewed
Step 5: Inviting Comparison	Teacher's comment on the work is non-specific, evaluative (e.g., this is good, satisfactory, poor) rather than descriptive	Teacher comments on the work, referring to the assessment criteria	Teacher encourages students to reflect and comment on the work, referring to the assessment criteria
Step 6: Identifying Next Steps	Teacher provides general instructions for next steps	Teacher is directive, identifies next steps, and instructs students	Teacher encourages students to identify next step(s)
Step 7: Second Attempt	No second attempt offered	Students try again but are unclear about improvements needed	Students try again, clearly focused on what needs improvement and how to achieve it
Step 8: Students Looking Back	No attempt made to look back and recognize progress	Progress recognized but only in general terms	Teacher prompts students to recognize their learning and specific progress as a frequent routine, and over longer cycles of time

The intent can be explored after the task has been explained or even started: decisions about timing depend on the nature of the task, the learning preferences and profile of the students, and other circumstances.

**Learning profile *is defined as including the student's cognitive, affective, psychomotor domains, developmental level, and learning style.*

BIBLIOGRAPHY

Assessment Reform Group. *Assessment for Learning Beyond the Black Box.* Cambridge, UK: University of Cambridge School of Education [1999].

Black, P., and D. Wiliam. "Inside the Black Box: Raising Standards Through Classroom Assessment." *Phi Delta Kappan* 80, No. 2 (October 1998): 139–148.

Chappuis, S., and R.J. Stiggins. "Classroom Assessment for Learning." *Educational Leadership.* Association for Supervision and Curriculum Development (September 2002): 40–43.

Clarke, S. *Targeting Assessment in the Primary Classroom: Strategies for Planning, Assessment, Pupil Feedback and Target Setting.* London, UK: Hodder and Stoughton, 1998.

_____. *Unlocking Formative Assessment: Practical Strategies for Enhancing Pupils' Learning in the Primary Classroom.* London, UK: Hodder and Stoughton, 2001.

Costa, A., and R. Garmston. *Cognitive Coaching: a Foundation for Renaissance Schools.* 2nd. ed. Norwood, MA: Christopher-Gordon, 2002.

Costa, A.L., and B. Kallick. "Learning Through Reflection." In *Habits of Mind: A Developmental Series.* Book III, *Assessing and Reporting on Habits of Mind.* Alexandria, VA: Association for Supervision and Curriculum, 2000.

Davies, A. *Making Classroom Assessment Work.* Courtenay, BC: Connections Publishing, 2000.

Davies, A., C. Cameron, C. Politano, and K. Gregory. *Together Is Better: Collaborative Assessment, Evaluation, and Reporting.* Winnipeg, MB: Peguis Publishing, 1992.

Fogarty, R., and J. Stoehr. *Integrating Curricula with Multiple Intelligences Teams, Themes and Threads.* Palatine, IL: Skylight, 1995.

Gregory, K., C. Cameron, and A. Davies. *Knowing What Counts.* Vol. 1, *Setting and Using Criteria.* Courtenay, BC: Connections Publishing, 1997.

_____. *Knowing What Counts.* Vol. 2, *Self Assessment and Goal Setting.* Courtenay, BC: Connections Publishing, 2000.

_____. *Knowing What Counts.* Vol. 3, *Conferencing and Reporting.* Courtenay, BC: Connections Publishing, 2001.

Sutton, R. *Assessment for Learning.* Salford, UK: RS Publications, 1995.

_____. *The Learning School.* Salford, UK: RS Publications, 1998.

Stiggins, R. *Student-Centered Classroom Assessment.* 2nd ed. Columbus, OH: Merrill Publishing, 1997.

Wiggins, G. *Educative Assessment: Designing Assessments to Inform and Improve Student Performance.* San Francisco, CA: Jossey-Bass Publishers, 1998.

Wiggins, G., and J. McTighe. *Understanding by Design.* 2nd ed. Alexandria, VA: Association for Supervision and Curriculum Development, 2005.

Notes

Notes